Bible Basics
for
Praying
in the Presence
of God,
A Way of Life

1055

By
Ann Evans

Bible Basics for Praying in the Presence of God, A Way of Life
A ready reference manual for forming a positive relationship with God through prayer

SPECIAL EDITION
Copyright © 2008 by Ann Evans

ISBN 978-0-9822777-0-6
Printed in the United States of America

Unless otherwise indicated, Bible quotations are taken from the King James Version of the Holy Bible.

To order more copies of this book, request a free copy of CpC's monthly newsletter, inquire about author speaking engagements or any other concern please send correspondence to:

CpC Community Prayer Circle
Post Office Box 471
Attention: CpC Publications Department
Homewood, Illinois 60430
Email:communityprayercircle@comcast.net

Bible Basics
for
Praying
in the Presence of God,
A Way of Life

A ready reference manual for forming a positive relationship with God through prayer

By
Ann Evans

Editors
Mozella Smith
Shirley Stewart
Brenda Szendroi

Cover Design by
William Sutton
of Eye-See Art Productions
in conjunction with
Darrow Alexander
of Below Zero Graphics

CpC Publishing
Homewood, Illinois 60430

A Prayer of Thanks and Request for Blessings

Our Father, God in Heaven, God of mercy, and grace, all honor and glory is Yours. All righteousness, peace, joy in the Spirit and power come from You. Thank You, for the vision to write this book. Thank You, O my Father Lord and Savior for all those You have put in my path to support this endeavor. Bless them according to Your loving kindness and riches in glory. Praise Your Name. Thank You, for the encouragement given from family, friends, CpC members, distant associates and at times even strangers. Keep them forever in Your care. Thank You for holding me up when challenges of this undertaking sought to bring me down. Thank You. You are faithful and true. You have unfailing love. Holy is Your Name. By Your grace and mercy this book is written. May Your will be done for each reader. Bless each of us to communicate with You continually. Bless each of us to live a life style tightly woven with prayer at Your Throne of Grace. Keep us from the wiles of evil one. Let each of us grow in Your grace, power and strength. Let Your Kingdom come in our lives. For You are the Power and the Glory forever, in the precious name of Jesus, I pray.

Amen

Contents

Dedications

To Curtis my beloved husband, your firm support and kind heart encouraged me to continue writing regardless of the many obstacles encountered prior to the completion of this book.

To Aunt Mary Green, the family rock, who abounds with never ending love.

To Miriam Lykke, your kindness and unfailing support are beyond words to describe.

In recognition of my mother, Ella, and my two supporting aunts, Lillie and Annie, all resting in peace „til Jesus returns.

To those above who remain, respectfully I dedicate this book, with all praises to God, my Father, Jesus my Savior, and the Holy Ghost, my guide.

Acknowledgements

All praises to God for the vision and completion of this book. Thanks to Mary King, MaryAnn Shaunnessey, Mozella Smith, Shirley Stewart, Brenda Szendroi, members of the entire CpC community and all who have dedicated their time, energy and prayers to help make this vision a reality. There are no words to express my gratitude to each of you for your kindness and faithful service. Your diligence in editing, proofreading, words of encouragement and financial assistance shall never be forgotten.

Thank you.

Reviews

"I sincerely recommend the reading and use of this book as: a prayer tutor in text, a prayer journal guide, and a prayer study reference for all prayer warriors and prayer groups."
Rev. Keith E. Davenport, Founder/Pastor
Results Plus Ministries, Inc.
Results Plus Ministries Christian Center
Email: rpmresults@msn.com

"After sixty years of ministry, I wouldn't add or subtract anything from this book. Well done!"
Rev. Donald Ganstrom, Retired
North American Baptist Association
Oak Brook Terrace, Illinois.

"… very interesting. The writer did some outstanding research on prayer. The reading of this book is sure to increase the development of one's prayer life."
Rev. James Love,
Love Tabernacle
Maywood, Illinois

"This book depicts more than asking for things… It is a wonderful tool that may empower our prayer lives and enhance our scripture memory. It reminds us that prayer should be mixed with praise and thanksgiving all to the glory of God."
Rev. Victor Pope, Associate Minister,
Bethlehem Temple Missionary Baptist Church
Harvey, Illinois

"Bible Basics for Praying in the Presence of God, A Way of Life, is a practical book that will make every Christian's prayer life more enriched and fulfilling. Topics strategically sequenced, guide the reader through many questions that are common among praying people. Without question, this book will enhance your knowledge about prayer and your spiritual prayer life."
Rev. Dr. Reginald J. Saffo,
United Faith Christian Institute Bible College
Maywood, Illinois

"Reading this book will strengthen your relationship with GOD and will help you understand the principles and the importance of praying in HIS presence."
Rev. Jeffery Smith, Assistant Pastor,
Bethlehem Temple Missionary Baptist Church
Harvey, Illinois

"I found Bible Basics for Praying in the Presence of God, A Way of Life by my friend, Ann Evans, to be a very enjoyable synopsis on prayer life. Ann offers scriptural teaching on prayer to speak loud and clear. Her insights will be helpful in a practical way to anyone who is seeking to cultivate a deeper life of prayer with God."
Pastor David Steinhart, Senior Pastor,
Forest Park Baptist Church
Forest Park, Illinois

"Praise God, for the writing of this book."
Paula Cook, Women's Prayer Group
Chicago Church of The Nazarene
Lemont, Illinois

Introduction

"I pray for them: I pray not for the world,
but for them which thou hast given me;
for they are thine.... Neither pray I for these
alone, but for them also which shall believe on me
through their word; That they all may be one; as
thou, Father, art in me, and I in thee, that they also
may be one in us: that the world may believe that
thou hast sent me.
And the glory which thou gavest me I have given
them; that they may be one, even as we are one: I
in them, and thou in me...,"
John 17:9, 20-23a

Because Jesus prayed for us to God, our Father,
we can pray to God, our Father, through Jesus,
our Lord and Savior, the Christ.
Curtis Evans

As time passes, and man grows farther and farther away from the will of God, culture and tradition play a major influence on the perception of prayer. At one time in American history, most Americans took it for granted that men should always pray to our God and Father in Heaven. In our present general lifestyle, seldom is prayer considered a way of life. Prayer in our society has become too cumbersome for some, too mystical for others and just unnecessary for countless more. Prayer is not cumbersome. It is not mystical.

Neither is prayer unnecessary. It is vital for all believers. In fact, prayer is the essential means to talk with God on a regular basis.

For some reason, many tend to hold to the misguided premise that effectual fervent prayer in the presence of God at His Throne of Grace must be laborious, lengthy or only designed for the godly elite. Some feel it is imperative to weave in several specific verses from the Bible while praying. Various others are inclined to believe that prayer can only be effective if it incorporates a special pitch or sound of voice when spoken aloud. They also believe this behavior is a feat that only the 'chosen' can accomplish. These assumptions are frequently traditional and often cultural. Not one of them is biblical. Actually, not one of these assertions can be substantiated in the entirety of The Holy Bible.

Several devout church attendees are emphatic about their reasons for not praying. Some have identified prayer as a gift they do not have. Please know that prayer is an innate quality given to everyone by God. It is a privilege for all mankind. Others have stated that God knows their heart, therefore they need not pray.

"for I know their imagination which they go about, even now,"
Deuteronomy 31:21c

Even so, prayer is necessary for all believers to:

1)   connect with God and
2)   do His will for His Glory.

Still others have stated they feel uncomfortable when they make an effort to pray. It is true; our righteousness is as dirty, filthy rags before God without Christ. This indeed may make us uncomfortable when coming to the Throne of Grace in the presence of God.

"But we are all as an unclean thing, and all our righteousness are as filthy rags;..."
Isaiah 64:6

Nevertheless, we are encouraged to humble ourselves and pray.

"If my people, which are called by my name, shall humble themselves, and pray, and seek my face, and turn from their wicked ways; then will I hear from heaven, and will forgive their sin, and will heal their land."
2nd Chronicles 7:14

A sizable number, have made it known that they are living a God filled life and there has been no need to pray. How can one live a life filled with God without an exchange of thoughts, feelings, concepts and precepts with God? Can one truly have a life filled with someone with whom he never communicates? It is guaranteed that a relationship without communication will falter, if not fail completely. Consistent communication is vital for a strong positive relationship of any kind. Without prayer, there can be no growing relationship with God.

"Whom shall he teach knowledge? and whom shall he make to understand doctrine? them that are weaned from the milk, and drawn from the breasts. For precept must be upon precept, precept upon precept; line upon line, line upon line; here a little, and there a little:"
Isaiah 28:9-10

Gradually weaned from the milk, and systematically taught, one-step at a time; the doctrine of God through Jesus Christ will be learned. The knowledge of God, His doctrine and His precepts are encouraged as a positive prayer life is developed. Strength and maturity come as communication with God continues. One cannot live a God filled life without a consistent prayer life.

Even more have spoken their belief that staying on a prayer list at church or in some other prayer group makes their prayer life complete. Yes, intercessory prayer is good.

12

"For God is my witness, whom I serve with my spirit in the gospel of his Son, that without ceasing I make mention of you always in my prayers;"
Romans 1:9

Nevertheless, it is also necessary for believers to pray for themselves as well as others.

"Be kindly affectioned one to another with brotherly love; in honour preferring one another; Not slothful in business; fervent in spirit; serving the Lord; Rejoicing in hope; patient in tribulation; continuing instant in prayer;"
Romans 12:10-12

Each Christian must have a personal relationship with God. A relationship with God through Jesus Christ may not occur without ongoing and continual prayer.

If you have felt any of the above assumptions, if any of these thoughts have crossed your mind, or if any of these impressions are of interest to you, Bible Basics for Praying In the Presence of God, A Way of Life is the book for you. It is anticipated that this book will provide sound principles on fervent, effective prayer for the reluctant as well as the enthusiastic pray(er). For your convenience, scriptures taken from the King James Version of the Bible are inserted at each biblical precept as it is developed. Bible Basics for Praying In the Presence of God, A Way

13

of Life is a book for anyone who wants to develop a stronger relationship with God through Jesus Christ. Its purpose is to give relevant examples on:

1)   what prayer is,
2)   why God wants us to pray,
3)   what God expects of us when we pray,
4)   some reasons for answered prayer.

Scriptures from the Bible or noteworthy reflections related to the specifics of this book start each chapter. A personal prayer concludes several chapters. Every chapter is designed to encourage the reader to exercise his or her privilege to pray to our Father, *The Living God.*

"And it shall come to pass, that before they call, I will answer; and while they are yet speaking, I will hear."
Isaiah 65:24

An unwavering relationship with God through prayer can be developed. Prayer allows one to know and exercise God's will in daily life. Prayer can help one live a God driven life.

"Pray without ceasing. In everything give thanks: for this is the will of God in Christ Jesus concerning you"
1ˢᵗ Thessalonians 5:17-18

Our prayer for you is that God bless you to persevere in developing a full and meaningful relationship with God our Father, through prayer as a way of life. We pray that you meet in fellowship with other Christians. We pray that you read and meditate on His word, <u>The Holy Bible.</u> We pray that you pray with and for others. We pray that God execute His peace and joy in your life. We pray that you press on toward the mark of a high calling in Christ, Jesus. We pray that you do not fall into traps of negative attitudes, wrong motives, and hindrances of prayer. We pray that you develop good prayer habits. We pray that you enter His presence before His Throne of Grace with reverence, praise, and thanksgiving. We pray that you use your God given privilege to communicate with Him daily. We pray that your communication with Him help you mature in His grace and mercy in every aspect of your life. We pray that prayer becomes a way of life for you.

Believe that you can come into the presence of God. Believe that God answers prayer. Believe that prayer is a way of life.
Curtis Evans

The Model Prayer Often Called
The Lord's Prayer

"After this manner therefore pray ye:

Our Father which art in heaven,
Hallowed be thy name.
Thy kingdom come.
Thy will be done in earth, as it is in
heaven.
Give us this day our daily bread.
And forgive us our debts,
as we forgive our debtors.
And lead us not into temptation,
but deliver us from evil:
For thine is the kingdom,
and the power,
and the glory,
for ever.
Amen".
Matthew 6: 9:13

Chapter 1
Definition of Prayer

"...shew me now thy way,
that I may know thee..."
Exodus 33:13c

Prayer is the earnest act of verbal or silent communication with God. It is a discourse or exchange of understanding between God and the pray(er). Prayer is being in the presence of God, at His Throne of Grace, with confidence as reverence, thanksgiving, needs and desires are communicated to Him.

"And this is the confidence that we have in him, that, if we ask any thing according to his will, he heareth us:"
1st John 5:14

Prayer is as an expression of feelings, thoughts and ideas between man and God. These expressions may be audible or soundless. They may be in groups or they may be in solitude. Such dialogue is a phenomenon secured in faith.

"Now faith is the substance of things hoped for, the evidence of things not seen."
Hebrews 11:1

Faith is the realization of hope proven by Godly truth. Faith is the four seasons confirmed by seedtime and harvest, cold and heat, drought and rain, summer and winter, and day and night. It is as sure as lightning before thunder and shadows at high noon. Faith caused Abel to offer unto God a more excellent sacrifice than Cain did. It is faith that translated Enoch to God without seeing death. Faith is Abram's move from Ur of the Chaldeans to a land shown to him by God. It is faith that caused the daughter of Pharaoh in Egypt to find Moses after his parents hid him for three months. Faith is a heart-to-heart truth of God. It is unreserved surrender to the will of God, a trust and confidence in God's will for each believer. It is the believer's certainty that things hoped for within the will of God will happen. Faith is total mind body and soul acceptance to the truth of God, past, present and a time to come. Faith knows that God's will is the preeminent of all possibilities. In brief, faith is God's truth revealed to man and man's wholehearted acceptance of the same. Prayer in faith is a God given privilege. It gives man an opportunity to have access to God's presence at His Throne of Grace.

"But without faith it is impossible to please Him: for he that cometh to God must believe that He is, and that He is a rewarder of them that diligently seek him."
Hebrews 11:6

Faith purifies the heart. *(Acts 15:9)* The righteousness of God comes by faith. *(Romans 3:22)* It is faith that justifies the heathen. *(Galatians 3:8)* The just shall live by faith. *(Galatians 3:11)* Such phenomena, inexplicable to world logic, acknowledge and exemplify our dependence on God our Creator in every walk of life. Prayer through faith provides a channel for God's direction for our lives every hour of the day.

"I will therefore that men pray everywhere, lifting up holy hands, without wrath and doubting. (but in faith)"
1ˢᵗ Timothy 2:8

God communicates with man through his faith in Him. Every believer has a portion of faith.

"...God hath dealt to every man the measure of faith."
Romans 12:3d

Accompanied with prayer, faith is the fiber that manifests God's will as the solution for all problems and concerns in the life of believers. Prayer without faith is useless babble and never reaches the throne of God's grace.

If prayers are to be answered, the pray(er) must have a believing heart. The prayer(er) must have trust and unswerving confidence in God at all times. When communicating with God, faith and prayer are inseparable.

"...For He is Lord of lord's and King of kings and they that are with Him are called and chosen, and faithful."
Revelation 17:14c

Prayer is essentially a Christian responsibility. A primary means of Christian growth is developed through prayer. A prayer-less believer identifies a Christian as one with stunted growth. Therefore, prayer must include the involvement of two beings:

1)   <u>God</u> (The Triune God, The Holy Trinity)
    a.   The Creator of heaven and earth,
    b.   The Heavenly Father of Abraham, Isaac, and Jacob,
    c.   The Father of Jesus Christ, His only begotten Son and Savior for all.
2)   <u>man, woman and child</u>
    a.   created by God in His own image,
    b.   for His glory.

By means of prayer, Christians can transcend spiritually to the Throne of Grace, and immediately find themselves in the presence of God.

"Let us therefore come boldly unto the throne of grace that we may obtain mercy, and find grace to help in time of need."
Hebrews 4:16

Prayer is a transforming element for all Christians. It is the mechanism God has provided for man to contact and maintain a relationship with Him. The process established by God for a two-way exchange of information is prayer that transforms. That is, prayer changes the lives of Christians. It renews minds. It helps maintain the heart of a sinner saved by the grace of God, to do the will of God, for the glory of God.

Specifically, prayer involves mental stimuli that provoke a heartfelt language spoken or silent. It is a two-way exchange of information that creates an interactive fellowship between God and man. It entails an understanding that encourages man's submission to the will of God. Prayer actualizes the realization that God will respond from a variety of choices best suited for the situation or circumstance at hand.

Prayer in the presence of God is unlike any other form of communication. This communication granted through God's only begotten Son, Jesus, the Christ, and by the guidance of the Holy Spirit is a privilege to all believers. Linked together with faith, total trust and belief in God through His Son, Jesus, by the power of the Holy

Spirit prayer provides an opportunity to speak to God.

"... let him ask in faith, nothing wavering. For he that wavereth is like a wave of the sea driven with the wind and tossed. For let not that man think that he shall receive any thing of the Lord." James 1:6-7

Prayer is the expression of a sincere heart in communication with God. Prayer combined with faith in God can and does allow one to enter into the presence of God at His Throne of Grace. God is always available to hear prayers of faith.

"The Lord is nigh unto all them that call upon him, to all that call upon him in truth." Psalm 145:18

Chapter 2
The Purpose of Prayer

*"I exhort therefore,
that, first of all, supplications, prayers,
intercessions, and giving of thanks, be made for
all men; For kings, and for all that are in
authority; that we may lead a quiet and
peaceable life in all godliness and honesty."*
1ˢᵗ Timothy 2:1-2

The purpose of prayer is multifaceted and is an integral part of the Christian's way of life. Effectual, fervent prayer in the presence of God at His Throne of Grace must be intertwined with the believer's everyday lifestyle and the essence of Christian belief. Listed below are six essential reasons for prayer.

1. First and foremost, we pray to glorify God through His son, our Lord and Savior, Jesus Christ.

"And whatsoever ye shall ask in my name, that will I do, that the Father may be glorified in the Son."
John 14:13

"If ye abide in me, and my words abide in you, ye shall ask what ye will, and it shall be done

23

unto you. Herein is my Father glorified, that ye bear much fruit; so shall ye be my disciples."
John 15:7-8

"Let your light so shine before men, that they may see your good works, and glorify your Father which is in heaven."
Matthew 5:16

2.   We pray because God hears us when we pray.

"I cried unto the Lord with my voice, and He heard me out of His holy hill…"
Psalms 3:4

3.   We pray because God listens to us when we pray.

"Then shall ye call upon Me, and ye shall go and pray unto Me, and I will hearken unto you."
Jeremiah 29:12

4.   We pray because prayer is a means of achieving fellowship with God.

"That which we have seen and heard declare we unto you, that ye also may have fellowship with us: and truly our fellowship is with the Father, and with His Son Jesus Christ. And these things write we unto you, that your joy may be full."
1ˢᵗ John 1:3-4

5.   We pray because prayer offers possibilities for developing spiritual maturity.

"My son, despise not the chastening of the Lord; neither be weary of his correction: For whom the Lord loveth He correcteth; even as a father the son in whom he delighteth."
Proverbs 3:11-12

6.   We pray because God answers prayer.

"Call unto Me, and I will answer thee, and shew thee great and mighty things, which thou knowest not."
Jeremiah 33:3

These reasons for prayer illustrate the need of everyone to glorify God through prayer. The pray(er) is allowed to get to know the will of God for the fulfillment of a godly life as each one continues to pray.

During prayer, praise and thanksgiving are two ways to glorify God. To repent and ask forgiveness for sins and to forgive those who have sinned against you are means of submitting to God. These concepts must be actualized in sincere prayer.

God has definite conditions and guidelines for prayer. They are constantly mentioned throughout the Bible. Below are three scripture verses to remember regarding conditions and guidelines for prayer. Detailed specifics of this topic will be addressed in chapter five. For now, it is essential to know that there are fundamental conditions and specific guidelines for effective prayer.

"See that none render evil for evil unto any man; but ever follow that which is good, both among yourselves, and to all men. Rejoice evermore. Pray without ceasing. In everything give thanks: for this is the will of God in Christ Jesus concerning you."
1ˢᵗ Thessalonians 5:15-18

"Love your enemies, do good to them which hate you, Bless them that curse you, and pray for them which despitefully use you."
Luke 6:27b-28

"Let your moderation be known unto all men. The Lord is at hand. Be careful for nothing; but in everything by prayer and supplication with thanksgiving let your requests be made known unto God."
Philippians 4:5-6

The above scriptures testify that God wants prayers to be without corruption, and evil motives. He encourages prayer without ill will, but with compassion for others and thanksgiving to Him. That is, you are to be thankful regardless of situations or circumstances. Offer a time of thanksgiving and reverence in every prayer. Be obliged in all situations and circumstances for the cause of Christ. Learn, (in whatsoever state you may find yourself,) to be grateful. *(See Philippians 4:11)* Hallow the name of God because He is Holy. Acknowledge your gratitude to the God of all gods, because He gave His only begotten Son that you should not perish, but have everlasting life. *(John 3:16)* Declare thanks to the God of heaven and earth, because He strengthens the weak and energizes the strong. Praise the God of compassion, because He is faithful and His caring kindness never fails.

"...give thanks at the remembrance of his holiness."
Psalm 30:4b

What is the reason for prayer? The following are the reasons we pray. Pray to glorify God through His Son, our Lord Jesus. Pray in reverence of the holiness of God. Pray because God encourages you to communicate with Him. He hears and answers prayer. Pray to grow and mature in God, the Creator of all things. Pray because prayer is a means of forming a positive relationship with God.

*Father, God in Heaven, Creator of Earth and
Master of the Universe, I come to Thee.
"Through Thy precepts I get understanding:"
(Psalm 119:104a)
"Thy word is a lamp unto my feet, and a light
unto my path."
(Psalm 119:105)
O Lord my God, "lead me in the way
Everlasting"
(Psalm 139:24b),
in the precious name of Your only begotten Son,
Jesus Christ. Amen.*

Chapter 3
<u>S</u>pecific <u>T</u>ypes and
<u>P</u>ositions for <u>P</u>rayer

O' Lord my God, in my lying down
and my rising up, with my head bowed down and
my hands lifted up, I will pray.
I will express my adoration, praise and thanks to
You. I will speak my petitions and intercessions
to You. I will offer my body as a living sacrifice
to You, which is my reasonable service.
You are my strong tower.
To You will I pray.

P rayer, the act of communicating, being
nurtured and guided by the Holy Spirit of God,
can be demonstrated in many forms. Journals,
songs, hymns, poems, group and individual
utterances, silent thoughts, or spontaneous
shouts, initiated by man and received by God are
all prayers. Each of these prayers may include
acts of submission, worship, requests for
guidance and assistance, confession, and
intercession. As there are essential reasons for
prayer, so are there essential manners and
conditions for prayer.

It is God's will for man to pray. Following
are a few prayer basics.

29

1) Prayer demands focus on *THE WILL OF GOD FOR MAN* and not focus on the will of man for God.

2) God listens to our prayers within His will.

3) The continual act of prayer will provide an opportunity for godly maturity and active fellowship with God.

4) Effectual, fervent prayer has a Godly affect on the pray(er).

5) Sincere prayer within the will of God places one in the presence of God at His Throne of Grace.

6) God answers prayer.

7) If the above are done on a continual basis, prayer becomes a way of life.

Types of Prayer
The Written Journal

One way to pray is by means of written prayer journals. Written prayer journals are prayers and responses recorded on the printed page. They are not a diary of events. They are not notes of religious activities nor are they an exercise in creative writing. Prayers written in a journal are sanctified communications with God. They may be prayers of adoration praise and thanksgiving, submission, petition, confession, intercession, or all and any combination of the above.

The major purpose of written prayers is to keep track of the communication between the pray(er) and God. Such prayers encourage the heart and allow the pray(er) to see in writing the blessings bestowed by the Almighty Creator of the Universe, God in heaven, the Great I AM. By reading and reflecting on them, it is sincerely possible to praise God in the words of the Scripture verse below:

"For Thou, O God, hast heard my vows: Thou hast given me the heritage of those that fear Thy Name."
Psalm 61:5

What an encouragement! How can you help but praise and thank God in prayer. He is forever loving and faithful.

Written prayer journals are a concrete visual reminder that you can enter into the presence of God at His Throne of Grace whenever you pray in sincere confidence focused on the will of Him who created you in His own image and made you heir to His Kingdom.

Prayers in the Form of Poems, Songs, and Hymns

Prayers of adoration in the form of poems, spiritual songs and hymns bring melodies to the heart and righteous joy to the soul. They can be invigorating inspirations while in the presence of

God at His Throne of Grace. They help provide the spiritual strength needed to go through routines and any situations that may arise in daily life. They show respect to God and always hallow His name. These prayers express love and devotion to God our Father, Jesus our Savior, and the Holy Spirit our comforter and guide.

The book of Psalms is filled with such prayers. In them are adulations that sincerely express man's simplistic knowledge of God's profound immensity.

"Let us come before His presence with thanksgiving, and make a joyful noise unto Him with psalms."
Psalm 95:2

"Serve the Lord with gladness: come before His presence with singing."
Psalm 100:2

The words such as the following stimulating song come to mind when thinking of prayers of worship, adoration and adulation.

Joyful, joyful we adore Thee. God of glory, Lord of love. Hearts unfold like flowers before Thee, Opening to the sun above. Melt the clouds of sin and sadness drive the dark of doubt away. Giver of immortal gladness fills us with the light of day.
Henry VanDyke, 1852-1933

This poem also comes to mind in respect and reverence to our God and Father, Creator of the Universe.

Lord of all being, throned afar
Thy glory flames from sun and star
Center and soul of every sphere
Yet to each loving heart how near.
Oliver W. Holmes, 1809-1894

More often than not, prayers of worship ask for nothing. They are not prayers of petitions. They are not prayers of intercessions. They are not prayers that request forgiveness or confessions of any kind. They do not request personal favors. They simply pour out love and adoration for Almighty God in complete submission to Him.

From time to time, when you are in the presence of God through prayer, you may be consumed by the joy of the Lord. Your soul may sing, "Hallelujah! Glorify the Name of God!" Every now and then, pray a prayer of worship through song. Or say a poem of praise and thanksgiving to God with true sincerity of heart. You may experience joy in your soul as you worship Him. Because, He encourages you to be merry as you worship Him in prayer.

"Make a joyful noise unto God, all ye lands:
Sing forth the honour of his name: make his

praise glorious."
Psalm 66:1-2

Spontaneous Prayers

Spontaneous prayers uttered or silent may include adoration *(worship)* praise and thanksgiving, petition *(request)*, confession *(admittance of sin and wrongdoings)*, intercession *(plea for others)*, submission *(the act of yielding your all to God)*. Spontaneous prayers are on-the-spot prayers. They are right now prayers. They may be done individually or in groups. They may be done in private or in public. They tend to focus on the immediate situation at hand. Spontaneous prayers offer little time for forethought. An example may be as simple as an accidental stub of a toe. "O God, help me;" or at the point of a collision, "Lord! Save me."

"Make haste, O God, to deliver me; make haste to help me, O Lord."
Psalm 70:1

Silent Prayers

Silent prayers are individual in nature but may include others. For instance, during times of worship when a pastor or prayer leader says, "Let us pray." At that point, all may pray in complete knowledge of others. In silence, only God knows the essence of each pray(er's) prayer. Remember, you do not have to make appointments to talk with God. He has made provisions for you to come into His presence continually and without reservation. Silent prayers can be the main source of anytime prayers. You can go into your secret closet and pour out your heart to Him anytime. He is always available to hear you.

"But thou, when thou prayest, enter into thy closet, and when thou hast shut thy door, pray to thy Father which is in secret; and thy Father which seeth in secret shall reward thee openly." Matthew 6:6

Prayers of Submission

A prayer of submission is the act of yielding completely to God. Submissive prayers always include supplication. Supplication is the act of presenting one's self totally to God. Submissive prayers are not always included in a general list of types of prayers. Nevertheless, prayers of this sort are a vital component when in the presence of God at His Throne of Grace as a way of life. Submissive praying is a requirement by God for all humanity. This kind of prayer helps develop a right relationship with God. It embraces at least three factors. These factors are vital to what is commonly called a sinner's prayer. The sinner's prayer is discussed later in the section titled, 'prayers of confession.'

1) Belief in the Lord Jesus Christ as the Son of God.

"For God so loved the world, that He gave His only begotten Son, that whosoever believeth in Him should not perish, but have everlasting life. For God sent not His Son into the world to condemn the world; but that the world through Him might be saved."
John 3:16-17

2) Confession of sin(s) to God

"For all have sinned, and come short of the glory of God;"
Romans 3:23

3) Total obedience, to God through His son, Jesus Christ

"That at the name of Jesus every knee should bow, of things in heaven, and things in earth, and things under the earth; And that every tongue should confess that Jesus Christ is Lord, to the glory of God the Father."
Philippians 2:10-11

Prayers of submission should not be overlooked nor omitted from communication with God. In The Model Prayer often called The Lord's Prayer, Jesus said,

"...Thy will (not my will) be done in earth, as it is in heaven."
Matthew 6:10b-c

Submission to God through Jesus Christ is the

way of Christian living for all believers. Even at His crucifixion, Jesus said,

"...not as I (Jesus, the Son) will, but as Thou (God, the Father) wilt."
Matthew 26:39c

Prayers Requesting Guidance and Assistance

Requests for guidance and assistance include at least two kinds of prayer to God. They are as follows:

1) Prayers of Petition

Prayers of petition are prayers of request or entreaty. These prayers ask God for the granting of a specific need or desire. They are appeals or pleas to God for something that is within God's will, for God's glory and for His benefits to us.

"And Jabez called on the God of Israel, saying, Oh that thou wouldest bless me indeed, and enlarge my coast, and that thine hand might be with me, and that thou wouldest keep me from evil, that it may not grieve me! And God granted him that which he requested."
1st Chronicles 4:10

"Remember me, O Lord, with the favour that thou bearest unto thy people: O visit me with thy salvation."
Psalm 106:4

Supplications are included in petition prayers. Before the crucifixion of the Son of God, our Lord and Savior Jesus Christ, supplications were animal offerings to God for His intervention in a variety of situations, and especially during a time of crisis. Today our supplications are no longer burnt offerings of animals. They are our very own selves, living sacrifices, in humble sincere submission to God's will. Paul in Romans 12:1 states:

"I beseech you therefore, brethren, by the mercies of God, that ye present your bodies a living sacrifice, holy, acceptable unto God, which is your reasonable service."

Prayers with supplications are prayers of petition that express behaviors demonstrating obedience and submission to the will of God. They are cries for God's will to rest, rule and abide in all situations. Paul suggests that we always pray with supplication.

"*Praying always with all prayer and supplica-* *tion in the Spirit, ..."*
Ephesians 6:18a

Petition prayers with supplication are serious, as all prayers should be. They should not be taken lightly or without regard for the reverence of God and His statutes. Read the example provided in 1st Samuel 13:3-13. Frivolous prayers with disregard for the rules of God can lead to serious consequences. Be steadfast and serious when presenting yourself to God as a living sacrifice, your reasonable service. Humbly accept God's preeminence over all possible solutions for all possible situations of life. Paul further states:

"Be careful for nothing; but in everything by prayer and supplication with thanksgiving let your requests be made known unto God. And the peace of God, which passeth all understanding, shall keep your hearts and minds through Christ Jesus."
Philippians 4:6-7

These verses clearly indicate that submission, and supplication are vital components of all prayers. True believers surrender their all to God in prayer through His Son, Jesus with thanksgiving, reverence and respect. By doing so, the blessings of God's peace will control the thoughts and feelings of all who believe.

2) Prayers of Intercession

Prayers of intercession may be prayers of praise and petition for others, always with supplication and submission. A prayer of intercession is a spiritual privilege that allows one to come to the Throne of Grace in the presence of God on behalf of another. It is a prayer involving affairs other than the pray(er) for intervention in the concern at hand.

"Neither pray I (Jesus) for these alone, but for them also which shall believe on me through their word; That they all may be one; as thou, Father, art in me, and I in thee, that they also may be one in us: that the world may believe that thou hast sent me."
John 17:20-21

Intercessory pray(ers) are often called, '*Prayer Warriors.*' Prayer Warriors are pray(ers) who advocate in prayer to God our Father for others. They are men and women of God who devote the majority of their prayers for the well-being of others. Prayer Warriors of the Old and New Testament may be identified as the following: *(these are but a few prayer warriors identified in the word of God.)*

1) Abraham
"And Abraham drew near, and said, Wilt thou (God) also destroy the righteous with the wicked?"
Genesis 18:23

2) Moses
"And the Lord was very angry with Aaron to have destroyed him: and I(Moses) prayed for Aaron..."
Deuteronomy 9:20

3) Nehemiah

"I pray before thee (God our Father) now, day and night, for the children of Israel..."
Nehemiah 1:6d

4) David

"But let all those that put their trust in Thee rejoice: let them ever shout for joy, because Thou defendest them: let them also that love Thy name be joyful in thee. For Thou, Lord, wilt bless the righteous; with favour wilt Thou compass him as with a shield."
Psalm 5:11-12

5) Paul

"For God is my witness, whom I (Paul) serve with my spirit in the gospel of His Son, that without ceasing make mention of you always in my prayers;"
Romans 1:9

6) James

"Is any sick among you? <u>let him call for the elders of the church; and let them pray over him</u>, anointing him with oil in the name of the Lord: And the prayer of faith shall save the sick, and the Lord shall raise him up; and if he have committed sins, they shall be forgiven him."
James 5:14-15

7) Jesus Christ

"...I (Jesus, the Son of God) pray not for the world, but for them which thou hast given me; for they are Thine."
John 17:9

Jesus, with kindness and compassion, sieves our prayers as flour for a fine cake and intercedes to God, our Father, for grace and mercy upon those who offer themselves as living sacrifices of pure heart, right motives and attitudes, within God's will.

"...It is Christ that died, yea rather, that is risen again, who is even at the right hand of God, who also maketh intercession for us."
Romans 8:34

God does hear the prayers of intercessors for others. But never forget that it is Jesus, The Great Almighty Intercessor who intercedes to God for the prayers and supplications of the prayer warriors who pray for others.

Prayers of Confession

A prayer of confession is a prayer that agrees with God that personal sin has occurred. Confession prayers admit sins to God with a submissive, contrite and repentant heart with total supplication.

"I acknowledged my sin unto thee, and mine iniquity have I not hid...."
Psalm 32:5a

Every Christian must pray a prayer concerning the confession of sin, not once but as often as personal sin occurs. Each sinner must be woefully sorry for wrongdoings. Without confession of sin, there can be no relationship with God, our Father. An initial prayer of this sort is often called, 'the **sinners prayer.**'

"I said, I will confess my transgressions unto the Lord; and thou forgavest the iniquity of my sin."
Psalm 32:5b

Prayers of confession, must also include forgiveness of transgressions against the pray(er). Confessions of sins in prayer and the ability to forgive others for their transgressions against the pray(er) go hand and hand. Sin cannot truly be confessed without the forgiving of others who have sinned against you.

"For if ye forgive men their trespasses, your heavenly Father will also forgive you: But if ye forgive not men their trespasses, neither will your Father forgive your trespasses."
Matthew 6:14-15

If we confess our sins, He is faithful and just to forgive us our sins, and to cleanse us from all

43

unrighteousness."
1ˢᵗ John 1:9

" ...what doth the Lord Thy God require of thee,
but to fear the Lord Thy God, to walk in all His
ways, and to love Him, and to serve the Lord Thy
God with all Thy heart and with all thy soul, To
keep the commandments of the Lord, and His
statutes, which I command thee this day for Thy
good?"
Deuteronomy 10:12-13

All prayers to God should be open expressions of
total submission and acceptance to His will. All
pray(ers) must realize that God's will is better
than could ever be imagined by the thoughts of
man. No prayer should be presumptuous, but
always in humble obedience to the will of our
Father, for His glory. David prayed this prayer
for guidance and freedom from iniquity.

"Order my steps in thy word: and let not any
iniquity have dominion over me."
Psalm 119:133

Be prayerful that iniquity does not take control
over the life of anyone who believes.

Postures or Positions for Prayer

There are no precise postures or positions
for prayer prescribed in the Bible. However, the
following have been observed through the ages.
Each of them are acts of surrender and

solicitation for God's will in the life of the pray(er) as well as those being prayed for.

1) standing still,
2) standing while swaying the body,
3) kneeling,
4) sitting,
5) bowing on hands and knees,
6) laying down,
7) folded arms and hands,
8) hands clasped together,
9) hands lifted toward heaven,
10) holding hands with others,
11) touching others with hands.

A song comes to mind while discussing the positions and postures of prayer.

Father, I stretch my hands to Thee,
No other hope I know, If Thou withdraw
Thyself from me, Where shall I go?
Charles Wesley, 1891

Here are three expressions from the Old Testament that exemplify posture or positions for prayer.

Yadah: to hold out hands in reverence
Barak: to kneel in submission
Towdah: to extend hands in thanksgiving
Strong's Exhaustive Concordance, by James Strong

Worship God with these words and the mentioned gestures whenever possible.

Patriarchs and other Bible figures exercised a variety of positions when praying. They are as follows:

In the Old Testament
Moses and Aaron fell on their faces.
Numbers 16:22
Levites prayed while standing.
Nehemiah 9:4
Ezra and others prayed with lifted hands
and bowed heads with their faces to the ground.
Nehemiah 8:6
David meditated on his bed.
Psalm 63:6
David also sat before the Lord.
1st Chronicles 17:16
Solomon knelt with his hands spread upward toward heaven.
1st Kings 8:54
Ezekiel fell on his face and prayed.
Ezekiel 9:8
Daniel kneeled three times a day to pray.
Daniel 6:10

In the New Testament:
Jesus kneeled down.
Luke 22:41
Stephen at his death knelt to pray.
Acts 7:60

Peter kneeled down.
Acts 9:40
Paul prayed on bended knee.
Ephesians 3:14
Paul also requested that pray(ers) lift up Holy hands.
1ˢᵗTimothy 2:8

Based on the information provided, there seems to be several acceptable postures for prayer. Not one is more correct than another. However, kneeling is most often described when searching the Scriptures concerning postures and positions of prayer to God, our Father in Heaven. Know this: It is not the posture. It is the prayer that counts. God desires our communication with Him continually.

Evening, and morning, and at noon will I pray and cry aloud: and he shall hear my voice."
Psalm 55:17

"And call upon me in the day of trouble: I will deliver thee, and thou shalt glorify me."
Psalm 50:15

It is not the posture of the prayer.
You may kneel or you may stand,
when you come before the God who made man.
It's He who searches your soul
as your petitions for forgiveness of sin unfolds.
Do not be afraid to come before Him.

Never let His light that shines in you go dim.
You can pray here and you can pray there
because God can hear your prayer in any
position and anywhere.
Curtis Evans

~~~~~~~~~~~~~~~~~~~~~~~~~~~~~~~~~~~~

A Prayer of Petition and Adoration

Our Father, God in Heaven Creator of all things. Holy is Your Name. All praises and glory to You. You are God and beside You, there are none other. Your mercies are great and Your compassion fails not. Therefore, I beseech You O my God and Father to remove all obstacles of prayer from me. Cleanse me from my secret faults. Wash me thoroughly from all my iniquities. Cleanse my heart. Remove all carnality, uncertainty and unconcern in You from all my ways. Remove me from all presumptuous sin. Purge my unforgiving spirit. Purify my soul from strife, doubt and greed. Keep me from temptation and deliver me from evil. Humble my very being and renew a right spirit within me. Give me Your peace in all situations. Give me Your righteous in all circumstances and teach me Your way, so I may not sin against You or hinder my communication with You. Let Your will for me be my will and Your way for me my way.

Guide my steps in all that I do for Your honor and Your glory. You are my rock, my sword and my shield. You protect me and You lead me to the path of righteousness. You are my rock and my salvation. You are the source of all power and strength. You are my light in darkness. You are my shelter from a storm. You are my joy in the midst of sorrow. You are my comforter in chaos and my peace in conflict. Glory to Your Name. Hallowed is Your Name. Holy is Your Name Wonderful Counselor and Mighty God are You. I love You Lord. Bless me to love You more. My faith looks up to You. You are my eternal hope. For You are the kingdom, the power and the glory for now and forever more. Let nothing keep me from Your love; in Jesus name,

Amen.

~~~~~~~~~~~~~~~~~~~~~~~~~~~~~~~~~~~~~

A Prayer of Praise and Petition

My heart is fixed, O God, my heart is fixed: I will sing and give praise. My voice shall You hear in the morning, O Lord; in the morning I will direct my prayer unto You. Hear me, O Lord, when I cry, have mercy on me, and answer me. Lord, my God, create in me a clean heart and right spirit within me;
For Christ sake,
Amen.

A Sinners Prayer

Father, God, I am a sinner. I have trespassed against You and man. I repent of all my sins from the depths of my heart. Please forgive me. I confess with my mouth and believe Jesus is Your Son in my heart. I believe He was crucified for the atonement of my sins. I believe that the shed blood of Jesus is the ultimate sacrifice for all my sins. Please be my personal Savior through Your Son Jesus Christ. You said in Your word that if I confess with my mouth the Lord Jesus, and shall believe in my heart that You have raised Jesus from the dead I shall be saved.
Lord, I believe. Save me, in the name of Jesus. Amen

A Prayer of Praise and Thanksgiving

Our Father, Good, and Gracious and Almighty, Thank You, for allowing me the privilege to enter Your gates with thanksgiving in my heart; to enter Your courts with praise, to come before Your throne of grace and pour out my heart to You. For when I turn from my sinful ways and call upon You, You hear me. You answer my prayers and it doesn't matter where or what position I'm in when I pray. If my heart is fixed on You, You O Lord, God, my Father, will hear and answer my prayers. I magnify Your Name, I praise Your Name. Glory to Your Name. Thank You, God my Father in heaven for the privilege of prayer.   Amen

Chapter 4
Attitudes and Motives
for Prayer

"Create in me a clean heart, O God;
and renew a right spirit within me.
Cast me not away from Thy presence;
and take not Thy holy spirit from me.
Restore unto me the joy of Thy salvation;
and uphold me with Thy free spirit."
Psalm 51:10-12

It is essential to have right attitudes *(frame of mind)* and right motives *(reasons for action)* when communicating with God. When you pray you must have supreme regard for the will and glory of God. It is imperative that you totally reveal and submit yourself to God as you pray to Him at His Throne of Grace. God's will and His way for you are revealed when you have right attitudes and right motives for prayer in complete submission to Him.

The entirety of the Bible is representative of God's will for you. God more often than not speaks to you through His word, <u>The Holy Bible</u>. Therefore, it is an advantage if Bible study and meditation *(a mental exercise that provides a time of reflection on the word of God for understanding and manifestation in your life)* on a regular basis is a part of the sincere pray(er's) daily way of living. Wrong attitudes and inappropriate reasons for prayer are hindrances in the life of a praying Christian. Prayers involving wrong thoughts and motives are prayers of hypocrisy.

"And when thou prayest, thou shalt not be as the hypocrites are: for they love to pray standing in the synagogues and in the corners of the streets, that they may be seen of men. Verily I say unto you, They have their reward."
Matthew 6:5

Prayer without right attitudes and right motives produce no practical life changing effect or godly results. They tend to be mere recitations or recitals of ineffectual words. They are identified as self-gratifying utterances. Prayers generated by negative frames of mind and ungodly reasons are frequently without reverence, or sincerity to our Creator. They do not demonstrate submissiveness to Him. They are not governed by obedience to Him. They never merit His presence. They seldom if ever reach the Throne of His Grace.

A positive mind-set, (attitude), or right motive, (reason for prayer) is one that agrees with God's precepts. Such prayers agree with God's laws, His statutes and commandments. God's commandments are guidelines for righteous attitudes and motives in all situations of life. Acknowledgement of and obedience to these commandments are good indicators, or starting points for learning and accepting God's will in the life of every believer. Positive motives and attitudes for prayer are strong indicators of sure communication with God at His Throne of Grace.

"...blessed are they that hear the word of God, and keep it. (maintain the conduct of it)."
Luke 11:28

Let us take a minute to go over the best-known commandments given to man by God through Moses, The Ten Commandments. These commandments may be divided into three categories.

1) The first four commandments contain and are related to specific allegiance to God. They specify prohibitions regarding the Deity of God.

2) Commandment five refers to respect and reverence to earthly parents, inferring that respect for both God and His creation, man, are a necessity for those who submit to His will.

3) The last five commandments are instinctively universal. They cut across all racial and cultural distinctions. These commandments are incorporated in all forms of social and govern-

mental rules and regulations here on earth. All of the above are not suggestions, but command-ments and should be adhered to strictly.

"Therefore shall ye observe all my statutes, and all my judgments, and do them: I am the Lord."
Leviticus 19:37

Below are the Ten Commandments in detail.

Allegiance to God

1) "Thou shalt have no other gods before me "
Exodus 20:3

Submitting to God's will makes it possible to have no other gods before Him. That is, no living things or inanimate objects should come before God. No other deity real or imaged is greater than God who made heaven and earth.

"For all the gods of the people are idols: but the LORD made the heavens. Glory and honour are in His presence; strength and gladness are in His place."
1st Chronicles 16: 26-27

No other gods before ME include, mother, father, sibling, children, cherished possessions and positions. Nothing should come between a believer and the love of God. First glorify God, and then all else will fall in place. Love God. Submit to Him totally. Remember His love is so great that He gave His only begotten Son, The Innocent Blood, for the redemption of all mankind who believe.

2) *"Thou shalt not make unto thee any graven image or any likeness of anything that is in heaven above, or that is in the earth beneath, or that is in the water under the earth. Thou shalt not bow down thyself to them, nor serve them: for I the Lord thy God am a jealous God, visiting the iniquity of the fathers upon the children unto the third and fourth generation of them that hate me;"*
Exodus 20:4-5

"I am the Lord: that is My Name: and my glory will I not give to another, neither my praise to graven images."
Isaiah 42:8

When submitting to God's will and His way, never make images intended for worship of other gods or heavenly beings. If for some reason graven images are presented, never bow to them. *(Read the third chapter of Daniel for an account of obedience to this commandment.)* God is a jealous God. He must be revered and respected every day in every way. His word is true and He has promised to place the sins of fathers who worship graven images upon their children, and their children's children at least until the fourth generation. The consequence of this trespass against this commandment of God, as you can see, may be long lasting.

Because you love Him and revere Him, you have unspeakable gratitude for the sacrifice of His Son. You are committed to do the will of God through Jesus, the Christ. God reminds you at the same time that He is merciful to thousands of them that love Him and keep His commandments.

"And shewing mercy unto thousands of them that love me, and keep my commandments."
Exodus 20:6

3)   *"Thou shalt not take the name of the Lord thy God in vain; for the Lord will not hold him guiltless that taketh His name in vain."*
     Exodus 20:7

Your attitude of submission to God's will, must include reverence and respect for His Name. God will not find anyone who defames insults or deprecates His Name guiltless.

"And he that blasphemeth the name of the Lord, he shall surely be put to death, and all the congregation shall certainly stone him: as well the stranger, as he that is born in the land, when

he blasphemeth the name of the Lord, shall be put to death."
Leviticus 24:16

For a detailed account of the above verse, read the entire 24th chapter of Leviticus. From it, you will know that you cannot take the name of God in vain. Positive attitudes and right motives in your relationship with God will encourage diligent esteem for His Name. Revere His Name. Hallow His Name. Praise His Name. Glorify His name.

Listed here are some words often used to identify and revere the name of God.

El-Shaddai	The Almighty God
El-Elyon	The Exalted One
El-Olam	The Everlasting God
Elohim	The Omnipotent God

The New Combined Bible Dictionary and Concordance by Charles F. Pfeiffer

4)   *"Remember the sabbath day, to keep it holy."*
      Exodus 20:8

Christians in remembrance of the resurrection of Jesus and in honor of the Sabbath, on the first day of the week, Sunday, take time to worship God formally. This day is hallowed and holy. On Sunday *(the Christian analogue of the Jewish Sabbath)* Christians commemorate and observe the Lord's Day in worship, holy activities and ceremonies. The Sabbath is a day proclaimed by God to be a day of no labor (unnecessary work).

In the New Testament, the Pharisees took this commandment to extremes by adhering to strict and rigid practices never really intended by God. Jesus Christ corrects their interpretation of the Sabbath in the 12th chapter of Matthew.

"And, behold, there was a man which had his hand withered. And they asked him, saying, Is it lawful to heal on the sabbath days? that they might accuse him. And he said unto them, What man shall there be among you, that shall have one sheep, and if it fall into a pit on the sabbath day, will he not lay hold on it, and lift it out? How much then is a man better than a sheep? Wherefore it is lawful to do well on the sabbath days."
Matthew 12:10-12

This day is a holy day, ordered by God to do no unnecessary work. It is not a day to be without compassion and concern for your fellowman. If on the Sabbath day, assistance of any kind is needed for the well-being of man, do it.

"Six days shalt thou labour, and do all thy work:"
Exodus 20:9

"And on the seventh day ye shall have an holy convocation; ye shall do no <u>servile work</u>.
Numbers 28:25

The Sabbath is not a day to charge people guilty for needed deeds performed on the day set aside for worshiping God. In the above scriptures, Jesus warns us not to go to extremes as we observe the Sabbath day. Needless to say, some things must be done on the Sabbath day. Some are police emergencies, fire rescue, and hospital needs.

Earthly Respect for Parents

5) *"Honour thy father and thy mother: that thy days may be long upon the land which the Lord thy God giveth thee."*
Exodus 20:12

Pray(ers) in the presence of God at His Throne of Grace have a mind-set and a way of life that honors and respects their earthly parents.

"And he that smiteth (fights with/ physically and/ or verbally) his father, or his mother, shall be surely put to death."
Exodus 21:15

"For every one that curseth (causes harm and humiliation) his father or his mother shall be surely put to death:"
Leviticus 20:9a

These verses indicate a serious consequence for disrespect to parents. They clearly show that such activity can shorten one's life.

"Hearken unto thy father that begat thee, and despise not thy mother when she is old."
Proverbs 23:22

Children are also encouraged not to reject their parents when they are old. At the point of death on the cross, Jesus sought care for His mother. He said these words.

"...Woman, behold thy son! Then saith He to the disciple, Behold thy mother! And from that hour that disciple took her unto his own home."
John 19:26-27

Commandments for Social Order

6)   "Thou shalt not kill."
        Exodus 20:13

"He that smiteth a man, so that he die, shall be surely put to death."
Exodus 21:12

Men who kill others shall not go guiltless. Murderers should be put to death as the scriptures indicate. Legitimate war is not included in this Commandment.

"...the murderer shall surely be put to death."
Numbers 35:16b (See chapter 5 Jesus forgives all sins.)

60

"Ye have heard that it was said by them of old time, thou shalt not kill; and whosoever shall kill shall be in danger of the judgment: But I say unto you, That "whosoever is angry with his brother without a cause shall be in danger of the judgment:"
Matthew 5:21-22a

Jesus goes a step further. He says to be angry with your brother *(anyone or any group of people)* without a cause is also a concern worthy of judgment. *(See wicked imaginations in chapter five.)*

7)   *"Thou shalt not commit adultery."*
      Exodus 20:14

"And the man that committeth adultery with another man's wife, even he that committeth adultery with his neighbour's wife, the adulterer and the adulteress shall surely be put to death."
Leviticus 20:10

"Ye have heard that it was said by them of old time, thou shalt not commit adultery: But I say unto you, That whosoever looketh on a woman to lust after her hath committed adultery with her already in his heart."
Matthew 5:27-28

Even the thought of adultery is a sin. Do not get involved in the actual act or the thought of committing adultery. Additionally do not get involved with fornication *(unmarried sex)*, pornography*(indulgence in sexually explicit materials)* or other sexual acts outside of the will of God. Do not even think about it.

"Whither shall I go from thy spirit? or whither shall I flee from thy presence? If I ascend up into heaven, thou art there: if I make my bed in hell, behold, thou art there. If I take the wings of the morning, and dwell in the uttermost parts of the sea; Even there shall Thy hand lead me, and thy right hand shall hold me. If I say, Surely the darkness shall cover me; even the night shall be light about me. Yea, the darkness hideth not from thee; but the night shineth as the day: the darkness and the light are both alike to thee."
Psalm 139:7-12

"And why wilt thou, my son, be ravished with a strange woman, and embrace the bosom of a stranger? For the ways of man are before the eyes of the Lord, and he pondereth all his goings.
Proverbs 5:20-21

God knows your heart. He knows your comings and your goings. Wherever you are and whatever you do, the eyes of the Lord are upon you.

"The Lord is in his holy temple, the Lord's throne is in heaven: his eyes behold, his eyelids try, the children of men."
Psalm 11:4

He sees all and knows all. You cannot hide your disobedience and sins from Him.

8)　*"Thou shalt not steal."*
　　Exodus 20:15

A thief is one who deliberately takes that which is not his. A thief is a robber, a burglar, a shoplifter, a pickpocket, a bandit, a crook, an internet pirate or an identity thief. He preys on the easily beguiled and gullible. He steals. A thief is in violation of God's eighth Commandment. In most societies, a thief is detestable. God in Exodus 22:2 says,

"If a thief be found breaking up, (burglarizing) and be smitten that he die, there shall no blood be shed for him."

In this verse, God shows no mercy for a thief. If a thief is caught stealing and is killed in the process, no one should be blamed. The thief's death in such cases is justifiable. Here is a verse to consider concerning thievery.

"Let him that stole steal no more: but rather let him labour, working with his hands the thing which is good, that he may have to give to him that needeth."
Ephesians 4:28

If you desire to enter God's presence at His Throne of Grace, do not steal. Petition in prayer to God for everything you need, want and desire. Give an honest day's work for an honest day's pay. Give to others as you have prospered. With God as your supplier, you have no need to steal.

"But my God shall supply all your need according to his riches in glory by Christ Jesus." Philippians 4:19

9) *"Thou shalt not bear false witness against thy neighbour." Exodus 20:16*

As mentioned before, there are serious consequences for those who are disobedient to God's commandments.

"If a false witness rise up against any man to testify against him that which is wrong; Then both the men, between whom the controversy is, shall stand before the Lord, before the priests and the judges, which shall be in those days; And the judges shall make diligent inquisition: and, behold, if the witness be a false witness, and hath testified falsely against his brother; Then shall ye do unto him, as he had thought to have done unto his brother:"
Deuteronomy 19:16-19a

A false witness is a liar, a slanderer and a perjurer. The intent of a false witness is to deceive. A false witness is akin to a thief in that, a false witness is capable of swindling his prey.

In such situations, a false witness may suffer the same punishment as one who steals. In the scripture above, a false witness is to receive the same punishment proposed for the victim of lies. Read the book of Esther and see how the above scripture is manifested. Do not slander, commit perjury against your neighbor or speak lies. It is the goal of a sincere communicator with God to:

"...lead a quiet and peaceable life in all godliness and honesty. For this is good and acceptable in the sight of God our Saviour;"
1ˢᵗ Timothy 2:2b-3

The last of the Ten Commandments is frequently referred to as the secret sin because unless the thought is actualized, this infringement of God's commands often may not be seen or detected by others. But it eats at the very soul of the one who participates in this violation of God's Commandment.

10) *"Thou shalt not covet thy neighbour's house, thou shalt not covet thy neighbour's wife, or his manservant, or his maidservant, or his ox, or his ass, or anything that is thy neighbour's."*
     Exodus 20:17

Covetousness is defined as the unquenchable yearning or wanting something that belongs to someone else. It is an inordinate desire for another's possessions. Covetousness is closely associated with envy, jealousy and greed. Sometimes called, "Keeping up with the Joneses." Covetousness is a dangerous emotion. When actualized, it wreaks havoc in our society. Filled with deceit and treachery, it breaks down Christian character and throws righteousness and justice out the window. If left to fester, it generally manifests itself in malicious conduct.

Covetousness can cause sibling rivalry, family disputes, strife between neighbors, national antagonism, international incidents and world wars. The account of Cain and Abel falls in this category of sin. Cain was covetous both of God's acceptance of Abel's offering, and of Abel's relationship with God. Read the account of Cain and Abel in Genesis, chapter 4 of the Old Testament. David coveted Uriah's wife, Bathsheba. Because of his covetousness, David committed adultery with Bathsheba. To cover up his acts of adultery he ordered the death of Uriah in a deceitful way. O what a vicious web we weave when we practice covetous acts and attempt to deceive. Read 2nd Samuel chapter 11.

The old cliché, "The grass always looks greener" is a perfect example of the fundamentals of covetousness. The hearts of those who pray in the presence of God do not covet others, but instead they accept the will of God recognizing that no one can have anything greater than what God can give. God does not consider the selfish desires of man nor his abundance of possessions as a prerequisite for the gift of eternal life. So why covet?

"...Take heed, and beware of covetousness: for a man's life consisteth not in the abundance of the things which he possesseth."
Luke 12:15

God is able to give each one of us all we need, especially to do His service. Therefore, a Christian's heart should be set on obeying the commandments of God through Jesus, His Son. Our Triune God will take care of all believers. If you do His will, your desires will be met as long as they are in His will.

"Delight thyself also in the Lord: and he shall give thee the desires of thine heart."
Psalm 37:4

All infractions of these Commandments are ungodly, ugly and evil sins.

"For he (civil magistrate/the judge) is the minister of God to thee for good. But if thou do that which is evil, be afraid; for he beareth not the sword in vain: for he is the minister of God, a revenger to execute wrath upon him that doeth evil."
Romans 13:4

Believe it or not, our judges and governmental officers of the courts are given the power to act as ministers of God for our good. Obediently, they are to execute wrath upon them that do evil and violate the laws of God. *(Corruption of judges may be forth coming in another book. Don't be fooled, God is looking at corrupt judges and He will judge them accordingly.)*

Except for the grace and mercy of God through Jesus Christ, your sins will not go unpunished. It is by the innocent blood of Jesus that sins can be forgiven with full pardon.

"Thus speaketh the Lord of hosts, saying, Execute true judgment, and shew mercy and compassions every man to his brother:"
Zechariah 7:9

The Ten Commandments of God include a sense of fairness and, mercifulness, a lack of partiality and antagonism. The natural man cannot achieve these traits alone. The power of God is necessary for actualization of these righteous and godly behaviors. The fulfillment of these biblical attributes is directed from God through His son Jesus Christ. It is by God's love, goodness, grace and mercies through Jesus Christ *(His birth, life on earth, death, burial, resurrection, ascension and promise to return)* that keeps man from his sinful nature. Paul, inspired by God, puts this truth in the following words:

"For I delight in the law of God after the inward man: But I see another law in my members, warring against the law of my mind, and bringing me into captivity to the law of sin which is in my members. O wretched man that I am! <u>who shall deliver me from the body of this death? I thank God through Jesus Christ our Lord.</u> So then with the mind I serve the law of God; but with the flesh the law of sin."
Romans 7:22-25

Peter, an outspoken disciple of Jesus, stated:

"Blessed be the God and Father of our Lord Jesus Christ, which according to his abundant mercy hath begotten us again unto a lively hope by the resurrection of Jesus Christ from the dead, to an inheritance incorruptible, and undefiled, and that fadeth not away, reserved in heaven for you, <u>Who are kept by the power of God through faith unto salvation ready to be revealed in the last time.</u>"
1ˢᵗ Peter 1:3-5

As these scriptures indicate, it is by the power of God, His grace and His mercy that man has hope for attaining God's way for living. No man or woman can live God's way without God.

Over the centuries, since the sin of Adam and Eve in the Garden of Eden, man has grown farther and farther away from God and gradually developed psychological mechanisms that kept him from positively responding to God's will and God's way. Three common human defense mechanisms are detailed as follows:

Avoidance:

If the will and way of God seem adverse or tend to interfere with man's way of life, man simply avoids God's word and communication with Him. The Bible is not studied. Meditation on His word does not take place. In essence, the word of God is contrary to man's worldly frame of mind and actions. In this state, one usually tends not to congregate with believers. Often worship or Christian services are not attended. Prayer, communication with God, is void. Believers, be careful. Avoidance is a dangerous thing. Jonah made an attempt to avoid God and fell into the belly of a great fish. Do you think Jonah would have survived the digestion of the fish without the will of God in his life? Follow the will of God through Jesus Christ. The Bible encourages you to fellowship with other believers. It also promotes acts of love and good works toward fellow worshippers. Avoidance of congregating with believers and lack of prayer will surely distance one's communication with God.

"And let us consider one another to provoke unto love and to good works: Not forsaking the assembling of ourselves together, as the manner of some is; but exhorting one another: and so much the more, as ye see the day approaching. For if we sin willfully after that we have received the knowledge of the truth, there remaineth no more sacrifice for sins,"
Hebrews 10:24-26

Rationalizing:

If the will and way of God seem adverse and interferes with one's way of life, The Word is simply rationalized. The truth of God is bowed and bent in such a way as it becomes rational to sin for the good of the individual not the will of God. The reading and hearing of His word are deliberately *(and, many times while in a state of rationalization, subconsciously)* misinterpreted to suit his own desires. Prayer is rendered to change God's mind, not to do God's will. Although, God allows certain things in life to happen, man can never change God's will. Abram rationalized to call his wife Sarai his sister. Read what happened as a result of this rationalization in Genesis 12:11-20. Man's rationalization cannot compete with God's Perfect Will. Hear this. God says,

"For My thoughts are not your thoughts, neither are your ways my ways, saith the Lord."
Isaiah 55:8

"Thy word is true from the beginning: and every one of Thy righteous judgments endureth forever."
Psalm 119:160

"Be not deceived; God is not mocked: for whatsoever a man soweth, that shall he also reap. For he that soweth to his flesh shall of the flesh reap corruption; but he that soweth to the Spirit shall of the Spirit reap life everlasting."
Galatians 6:7-8

Denial:

If the will and way of God's word seem adverse to man and interferes with his own way of life, he simply denies the truth of God. In a like manner, if a model (family, friend or associate) of the will and way of God seem adverse to him and interferes with his own selfish way of life, he simply ignores the model and in essence denies God. Thus, he rejects the need to pray. When he hears scriptures such as the ones that follow, he does not attend to them. Due to his own selfish way of life, he rejects God. He ignores his models. He contradicts the scriptures and he does not pray.

"For the wrath of God is revealed from heaven against all ungodliness and unrighteousness of men, who hold the truth in unrighteousness;" Romans 1:18

"And even as they did not like to retain God in their knowledge, God gave them over to a reprobate mind, to do those things which are not convenient; Being filled with all unright- eousness, fornication, wickedness, covetous- ness, maliciousness; full of envy, murder, de- bate, deceit, malignity; whisperers, backbiters, haters of God, despiteful, proud, boasters, inventors of evil things, disobedient to parents, Without understanding, covenant breakers, without natural affection, implacable, unmerci- ful: Who knowing the judgment of God that they which commit such things are worthy of death.." Romans 1:28-32a

In this state of denial, one may frequently personalize and say God is too just for His wrath to be against "me" for what am I doing. ***"I'm"*** just living my life the way I want to. Who cares if ***"I'm"*** indifferent to the word of God? I'm hurting no one but myself.

Yes, that's just the problem. Living a life of denial of God's will and way for life is the way that leads to destruction and death. Denying God's will and His way will not make the truths of our God of heaven and earth go away.

Disobedience and denial God's will leads to death. Avoidance, rationalization or denial will never deter the reality of God, His truth and righteousness. God's word is true.

"For I am the Lord, I change not;"
Malachi 3:6a

"But whosoever shall deny me before men, him will I also deny before my Father which is in heaven."
Matthew 10:33

God is faithful. He offers the innocent blood of Jesus Christ His Son, as a ransom for the sins of man. Accept His will through His Son, Jesus Christ and be saved from the wrath of God.

O precious creation of **The Living God**, should you find yourself in a state of any one of these psychological defense mechanisms, submit yourself to God and pray for His will and His way in your life. By doing so, you glorify Him. His will for you is better than you may ever imagine. Do you believe this?

Human defense mechanisms absolutely inhibit you from entering in the presence of God at His Throne of Grace. The Bible throughout repeatedly shows that man of his own will cannot stop these negative traits. Under the influence of his own defense mechanisms, he will never be able to pray in the presence of God at His Throne of Grace with positive results. He must be kept by the will of God. God stands ready to accept all by the Innocent Blood of Jesus Christ, His Son, and the power of the Holy Spirit, the comforter and guide for all believers.

Believers are kept by the power of God through faith in Jesus. They are kept by the love of God through His Son. Through Him, all things are possible for those who believe. Believers can do all things through the strength He gives. It is by the grace of God, the power of the Holy Spirit and the love and mercy of Christ that believers are able to communicate with God in prayer.

"The Father loveth the Son, and hath given all things into His hand. He that believeth on the Son hath everlasting life: and he that believeth not the Son shall not see life; but the wrath of God abideth on him."
John 3:35-36

"There is therefore now no condemnation to them which are in Christ Jesus, who walk not after the flesh, but after the Spirit."
Romans 8:1

By faith, the love, and power of our Triune God, believers can overcome all defense mechanisms and other forms of disobedience to God's will. Through Jesus, believers can submit their total being for God's glory. The presence of God at

His Throne of Grace is open to all who have faith in God the Father in heaven. He is open to all who believe in Christ, the author and finisher of every believer's faith.

"Wherefore seeing we also are compassed about with so great a cloud of witnesses, let us lay aside every weight, and the sin which doth so easily beset us, and let us run with patience the race that is set before us, Looking unto Jesus the author and finisher of our faith; who for the joy that was set before Him endured the cross, despising the shame, and is set down at the right hand of the throne of God."
Hebrews 12:1-2

Are you a believer? If so, the sacrifice of Jesus allows your heart and mind to transform to newness in Him. This renewed mind or these renewed attitudes and motives place you in the presence of God at His Throne of Grace when you pray.

"I beseech you therefore, brethren, by the mercies of God, that ye present your bodies a living sacrifice, holy, acceptable unto God, which is your reasonable service. And be not conformed to this world: but be ye transformed by the renewing of your mind, that ye may prove

what is that good, and acceptable, and perfect, will of God."
Romans 12:1-2

Have you presented your body holy and acceptable to God, which is your reasonable service? Easier said than done, you say. You are correct! It is hard to break old habits and give up a lifestyle you enjoy regardless of how abominable it may be to God. It is hard to give up old selfish ways. In a world riddled with the concept, "be your own man (or woman) and get what you can, while you can, wherever you can, at the expense of anyone you can." Yes, it is hard to submit to a Holy Triune God, unseen by the naked eye, solely identified by faith. It is hard, but not impossible. Faith in God through Jesus Christ makes all things possible.

"...With men this is impossible; but with God all things are possible.
Matthew 19:26b

Consider this. Jesus, the Son of God, descended from a heavenly state to a lowly state on earth.

"B*ut made himself of no reputation, and took upon him the form of a servant, and was made in the likeness of men:"*
Philippians 2:7

77

At birth, **The Son of God,** was wrapped in swaddling cloth, *(bands of cloth wrapped around newborn babies to protect their posture)* and laid in a manger *(a place where farm livestock eat).* His earthly parents were common people. They had no wealth, no high-ranking social prestige or power. As a young child, He lived in Egypt as a safeguard against the brutal murder of all male children around His age by a Roman appointed King of Israel.

"Then Herod,... slew all the children that were in Bethlehem, and in all the coasts thereof, from two years old and under, according to the time which he had diligently inquired of the wise men (concerning Jesus, King of the Jews)."
Matthew 2:16

As an adult, He lived in a place called Nazareth of which the Bible states:

"...Can there be any good thing come out of Nazareth?..."
John 1:46b

His earthly father was a carpenter. He had earthly sisters and brothers. *(Matthew 13:55-56)* They held him with no special regard. He chose twelve men to help Him do the will of His heavenly Father, God, while here on earth. One of them betrayed Him. One of them denied Him. All of them initially refused to believe that He had risen from the dead, especially Thomas.

"And they, when they had heard that he was alive, and had been seen of her, believed not."
Mark 16:11

"...Except I (Thomas) shall see in his hands the print of the nails, and put my finger into the print of the nails, and thrust my hand into his side, I will not believe."
John 20:25b

Jesus honors this disciple's request.

"Then saith he (Jesus) to Thomas, reach hither thy finger, and behold my hands; and reach hither thy hand, and thrust it into my side: and be not faithless, but believing. And Thomas answered and said unto him, My Lord and my God."
John 20:27-28

Regardless of the attitudes or motives of His chosen, before His crucifixion for the sins of all men, Jesus turned water into wine. He healed the sick. He gave sight to the blind. He made the lame walk and the speechless talk. He cast out demons. He raised the dead. He had no sin. Yet He became the ultimate and final sacrifice for the atonement of sin for man. He gave His life.

"For He hath made Him to be sin for us, who knew no sin; that we might be made the right-

eousness of God in Him."
2nd Corinthians 5:21

He, the Son of our Living God, paid the sin debt for all who believe. For without His self-sacrifice, there would be no redemption or reconciliation for man with God. It was not easy for Him but He did it. The Bible says,

"And being in an agony He prayed more earnestly: and His sweat was as it were great drops of blood falling down to the ground."
Luke 22:44

No, it was not easy, but He did it. And because He did it, we have an opportunity to overcome our lustful, sinful, disobedient ways. O my dear friends, He could have decided a different way of life on earth. He could have prayed a different prayer. He could have decided not to sacrifice His life for us. He could have left us in our own unresolved state of sin, bound for the destination of eternal hell. But His love for us was so great that He gave His own life so we may have a chance to live for eternity with Him, in the kingdom of God. He calls all believers friend. What a blessing to be called a friend of Jesus, the One who died for us, the Son of God.

"Greater love hath no man than this, that a man lay down his life for his friends."
John 15:13

It was not easy for the Son of God, but He did it. Please remember, if a resurrection did not occur, everybody's prayers would be in vain. All praises to our Lord, and Savior, Jesus Christ for His action on the cross. It is because of Jesus that we can submit our lives to God, for His glory. Jesus has made it easy for us. He said,

"A new commandment I give unto you, That ye love one another; as I have loved you, that ye also love one another. By this shall all men know that ye are my disciples, if ye have love one to another"
John 13:34-35

You can overcome your frailties and come into the presence of God at His Throne of Grace when you sincerely believe in and obey this new commandment. By obeying this commandment, you can easily overcome the challenges of submitting to The Ten Commandments, statutes, and ordinances of God, for daily living in a life of fairness and mercy without partiality and/or antagonism. You can also overcome human internalized defense mechanisms designed to cover-up and disobey the will of God. If you do not believe this, try standing on the power of God and accept the commandment of Jesus in your heart right now, realizing:

81

"That your faith should not stand in the wisdom of men, but in the power of God."
1ˢᵗ Corinthians 2:5

The inspired word of God by His messenger Paul is clear.

"I can do all things through Christ which strengthened me."
Philippians 4:13

Another aspect of positive attitudes and right motives for prayer is humility. Humility is a behavior of meekness. The act of humility is the reverential confidence and trust in God with utmost modesty. It is not frailty or faintness of courage as often associated with weakness. Humility is in the heart of every Christian. It should be demonstrated during an act of fervent effectual prayer. James tells us to,

"Humble yourselves in the sight of the Lord, and he shall lift you up."
James 4:10

The book of Hebrews declares,

"Let us draw near with a true heart in full assurance of faith, having our hearts sprinkled from an evil conscience, and our bodies washed with pure water. Let us hold fast the profession of that promised;)"
Hebrews 10:22-23

Job explains,

"Though He slay me, yet will I trust in Him: but I will maintain mine own ways before Him. He also shall be my salvation: for a hypocrite shall not come before Him."
Job 13:15-16

Humbled pray(ers) will be lifted up. Confident pray(ers) will hold fast to the profession of their faith without wavering. Trusting pray(ers) have the salvation of God. The blood of Jesus, His grace, mercy and the power of the Holy Spirit will give you the privilege to stop thinking of ways to correct specific difficulties or problems in everyday life on your own. Instead, reliance on the Triune God occurs. By doing this, minds are renewed. Positive attitudes and good motives spring from within by the power of God through Jesus Christ. Concentrating on His will is eminent. When you humble yourself for His way in your life, you no longer toil over how to triumph adversities in your life. You know from where your help comes. You trust in Him with all your being. At this level of maturity in God, you can freely and without reservation let go and let God. You openly accept the Comforter Jesus has promised to every believer. You know to call on God, the Father. He will deliver you, if you are sincere with Him and submit to His will. You find joy in prayer to Him and confidence that He is with you all the time.

"And I will pray the Father, and he shall give you another Comforter, (The Holy Spirit) that he may abide with you forever;"
John 14:16

"And call upon me in the day of trouble: I will deliver thee, and thou shalt glorify me."
Psalm 50:15

"The Lord is nigh unto all them that call upon Him, to all that call upon Him in truth."
Psalm 145:18

"As for me, I will call upon God; and the Lord shall save me. Evening, and morning, and at noon, will I pray, and cry aloud: and He shall hear my voice."
Psalm 55:16-17

"Rejoice evermore. Pray without ceasing. In everything give thanks: for this is the will of God in Christ Jesus concerning you."
1ˢᵗ Thessalonians 5:16-18

When you call upon God through Jesus Christ with right attitudes and good motives, you can boldly come into His presence at His Throne of Grace for His glory as a way of life.

Chapter 5
Prayer Hindrances

"These six things doth the Lord hate:
yea, seven are an abomination unto him:
A proud look, a lying tongue,
and hands that shed innocent blood,
An heart that deviseth wicked imaginations,
feet that be swift in running to mischief,
A false witness that speaketh lies,
and he that soweth discord among brethren."
Proverbs 6:16-19

Abominations are definite obstructions to prayer. The abominations listed in Proverbs 6:16-19, the Seven Deadly Sins of Man, *(author unknown, but listed in the works of Pope Gregory The Great, born circa 540 and served in the Roman Catholic Church as Pope from 590-604)*, along with violations of the Ten Commandments are the essence of all hindrances to prayer in the presence of God at His Throne of Grace as a way of life. They are provocateurs of sin. They are loathsome to God. If prayer is to be a way of life for you, you must be able to detect these malefactors and flee from them.

The cares of this world delight in **lust**, gloat in **gluttony**, saturate in **slothfulness**, puff up with **pride**, overflow with **envy**, amplify **anger**, and ingratiate **greed**. These terms are dark traits identified as the Seven Deadly Sins of Man. All sins are deadly abominations. All abominations are in direct disobedience to God's Commandments. They are contemptible to Him. He does not tolerate them in His presence at His Throne of Grace.

God is a righteous and jealous God. He is adverse to all things contradictory to His will for mankind. Yielding to any one of the Seven Abominations stated in Proverbs 6:16-19, the Seven Deadly Sins, or disobeying the Ten Commandments given to us by God through Moses are totally and completely unacceptable to Him. Indulgence in these things without repentance, submission, and supplication to God's will is not overlooked when one comes in His presence before His Throne of Grace. The following detail hindrances to prayer as identified in the Seven Deadly Sins and Seven Abominations to God. The Ten Commandments have been discussed in chapter four.

Lust

In its simplest term, lust is an inordinate desire for bodily self-pleasure. This selfish desire is usually associated with sex acts. Lustful sex acts include:

Lasciviousness
lewd, vulgar, unchaste sexual activity

Fornication
consensual sex between those who are not married

Adultery
consensual sex with someone other than the marriage partner

Incest
Sexual activity among close relatives

Rape
forced sexual activity, and consenting sexual behavior between an adult and a minors

Pornography
Written, spoken, and visual material of an erotic nature intended to promote sexual excitement

Sodomy
unnatural, depraved sexual acts

All of the above are usually physical self gratifications without regard for morality, social codes of order, or Christian character. Lust easily attaches itself to pride, gluttony, covetousness, envy and greed. All of these are behaviors outside of God's will.

Lust, one of the most deadly of all sins is also among the most difficult to overcome. It can most definitely cause spiritual death. At times, it may be a key perpetrator of physical death as well. Lust contributes to crimes of passion, sexual diseases and moral decay in any society. Here are a few social concerns attributed to lust.

Divorce
Infidelity *(sexual unfaithfulness)* ranks third for the major causes of divorce.

Honor Killing
(cultural justification for murder due to violations of strict man-made rules and regulations) This behavior is not as prevalent as divorce but is usually found in spousal murders due to acts of lust.

Single Parents
Should trends prevail, a sizable number of children born in the twenty-first century may be reared by a single parent. The majority of which are products of sex among our youths (babies having babies).

STD's
Sexually Transmitted Diseases such as chlamydia, herpes, gonorrhea, syphilis, AIDS, HIV, etc.

This list could go on and on to including brothels *(places for male and female prostitutes)*, illegal abortions, and pedophilia to name a few more of the lustful behaviors that decay our moral environment. This sin is overwhelming in modern society. It sticks to hindrances of prayer like flies to fly paper. Such behaviors must not be tolerated among Christian believers.

On the bright side, American vernacular and idiom, at times, tend to identify lust as a positive trait such as *'a lust for learning.'* Lust, when used in a positive manner usually involves an enthusiasm and eagerness or determination for the good. Therefore, if the trait of lust is within you, let it be for the good. Have an eager enthusiasm for the love of Jesus Christ. Be fervent for Him to rest, rule and abide in your daily life. Be passionate in your obedience to God's commandments and His will for you. Let His way be your way. Let His will be your will. The word of God encourages you to:

"Flee also youthful lusts: but follow righteous-ness, faith, charity, peace, with them that call on the Lord out of a pure heart."
2nd Timothy 2:22

"Let not sin therefore reign in your mortal body, that ye should obey it in the lusts thereof."
Romans 6:12

"...Walk in the Spirit, and ye shall not fulfill the lust of the flesh. For the flesh lusteth against the Spirit, and the Spirit against the flesh: and these are contrary the one to the other: so that ye cannot do the things that ye would."
Galatians 5:16-17

Gluttony

Gluttony is a greedy, selfish and excessive desire for more than is needed. It is usually identified in terms of eating and/or drinking. But it is also observed in the gathering of material things as well. Gluttony and greed go hand in hand. Please note: not all overweight people experience the sin of gluttony. Some folks who seem overweight may not be gluttons at all, while average-weight and even some under-weight people can indeed be guilty of the sin of gluttony. Regardless of one's appearance, the sin of gluttony strikes a deadly blow at the spiritual and physical well-being of man. It stabs young and old alike. It physically deteriorates the body and spiritually demoralizes the soul.

"Brethren, be followers together of me, and mark them which walk so as ye have us for an ensample. (For many walk, of whom I have told you often, and now tell you even weeping, that they are the enemies of the cross of Christ: Whose end is destruction, whose God is their belly..."
Philippians 3:17-19a

"Know ye not that ye are the temple of God, and that the Spirit of God dwelleth in you?"
1ˢᵗ Corinthians 3:16

How can a spirit of gluttony coexist with God in

the same bodily temple? Gluttony is a hindrance to prayers in the presence of God at His Throne of Grace. Don't let it be found among believers. Listed on the next page are two of the most common illnesses due to overindulgence:

1) obesity:

"a condition in which the natural energy reserve, stored in the fatty tissues of the bodies is increased to a point where it is associated with certain unhealthy conditions and the increased likelihood of mortality. Obesity is a forerunner of several diseases such as:

    a)   cardiovascular diseases

    b)   diabetes (type 2)

    c)   sleep apnea

    d)   osteoarthritis"

Internet, Wikipedia, The Free encyclopedia @http://en.wikipedia.org

2) bulimia nervosa:

a serious eating disorder that occurs chiefly in females, characterized by

    a)   compulsive overeating,

    b)   induced vomiting,

    c)   laxatives,

    d)   diuretic abuse,

    e)   guilt, and

    f)   depression.

Merriam-Webster Online Dictionary @ http://www.merriam-webster.com/

The threat of heart disease (high cholesterol), the inability to produce appropriate amounts of insulin (diabetes), fear of death during sleep (sleep apnea), the loss of cartilage of the joints (osteoarthritis), guilt and depression surely hinder adequate physical growth and maintenance, which in turn provide a strong opportunity to decrease one's prayer life.

Those who are overweight due to over-eating tend to take gluttony lightly. However, gluttony can be a cause of an untimely physical death. It is a dangerous transgression. Do not be nonchalant about it. The indulgence of gluttony leaves no room for the Spirit of God to dwell in you. Your thoughts are consumed with ways and means of self-satisfying, over-indulgent appetites for food or other things contrary to the will of God. Lack of the Spirit of God within you is of serious concern. Without God, through Jesus Christ, the gluttons hope for entrance to the Throne of Grace in the presence of God, for prayer, salvation or many of the other privileges and blessings of God, is greatly narrowed.

"For the drunkard and the <u>glutton</u> shall come to poverty: and drowsiness shall clothe a man with rags."
Proverbs 23:21

The act of gluttony may have caused Esau to lose his birthright.

92

"...Esau, who for one morsel of meat sold his birthright."
Hebrews 12:16b

Just as lust in our modern day vernacular can have positive connotations, so can gluttony. *'He's a work glutton'*, meaning he is a hard worker, one who loves to work excessively, a workaholic. Sometimes these people are said to have a "Type A personality." Be careful here. Anything to the point of excess may turn out to be a hindrance to a successful prayer life. *(Have you ever heard of the Christian who was too busy serving to pray?)* Nevertheless, if gluttony is a part of your lifestyle, let it be a great desire to do the will of God. Trust in Jesus as your Lord and Savior with enthusiasm and pray for the blessings of God's will while in His presence at His Throne of Grace.

Slothfulness

Slothfulness is laziness, both physically and spiritually. It is the inclination to be over-indulgent when resting and relaxing. Granted, from time to time in this rush-rush, hustle-bustle, hurry-hurry, world it is important to remove self from the pressing responsibilities and obligations faced on a daily basis. Even Jesus from time to time took some rest.

"And when they had sent away the multitude, they took him even as he was in the ship. ... And

there arose a great storm of wind, and the waves beat into the ship, so that it was now full. <u>And he was in the hinder part of the ship, asleep on a pillow:...</u>"
Mark 4:36, 37-38a

The average person calls this time of rest a getaway, a vacation, a little R and R (rest and relaxation) or simply time-off. The slothful accept this time as a way of life. They are on a perpetual vacation. They shun an honest day's work for an honest day's pay. They demonstrate no understanding of the following concept.

Work the works of Him who made you
and pray your prayers to Him who hears you.
Your eternity with Jesus depends on it.
Curtis Evans

The slothful demand an extremely inactive life style. Health wise, a slothfully directed life contributes to a cluster of physical illnesses as does the sin of gluttony. In its most severe state slothfulness has been identified as weakness and wasting away of organs and other body parts due to lack of use.

It is documented repeatedly that youths in our current society are becoming more and more gluttonous and slothful, resulting in an overall shortened life span for many. The combination of the availability of fast foods and usage of the advanced technological way of living has surely contributed to slothfulness. Truly, modern technology is making it very easy to develop a nation of gluttons and sloths.

Slothfulness is akin to wastefulness. Generally, slothfulness and poverty accompany each other. Shame and mischievousness are also close relatives of the slothful. Slothful behaviors lead to violations of God's will for man. Read some verses on what the Bible has to say about a slothful man or woman below.

"He also that is slothful in his work is brother to him that is a great waster"
Proverbs 18:9

"Slothfulness casteth into a deep sleep; and an idle soul shall suffer hunger."
Proverbs 19:15

"The sluggard will not plow by reason of the cold; therefore shall he beg in harvest, and have nothing."
Proverbs 20:4

"He that gathereth in summer is a wise son: but he that sleepeth (the slothful) in harvest is a son that causeth shame."*
Proverbs 10:5

"The hand of the diligent shall bear rule: but the slothful shall be under tribute."
Proverbs 12:24

"As the door turneth upon his hinges, so doth the slothful upon his bed"
Proverbs 26:14

"...this we commanded you, that if any would not work, neither should eat. For we hear that there are some which walk among you disorderly, working not at all, but are busy-bodies. Now them that are such we command and exhort by our Lord Jesus Christ, that with quietness they work, and eat their own bread."
2ⁿᵈ Thessalonians 3:10b-12

"The sluggard is wiser in his own conceit than seven men that can render a reason."
Proverbs 26:16

From these verses, we can see that it is hard to change the sluggards will and way from being lazy. The slothful can be depended on to find a way out of work. At times, they may be too lazy to eat. On the other hand, it may seem that all they do is eat. Even seven good men cannot change the sluggard's mind about becoming industrious.

A lesson is learned from the behavior of the slothful. A participant in the art of slothfulness is idol. He snoozes and sleeps his life away. His diligence is non-productive; therefore, he often finds himself without basic needs. He is wasteful but always in want. He cannot be motivated to change his ways. Truly, slothfulness is a hindrance to prayer because often, the slothful is too sleepy, or too tired to pray! Slothfulness impedes the will of God in one's life and sets up barriers to do His commandments. It is a killer, both physically and spiritually. Let slothfulness not be found among Christians.

"Go to the ant, thou sluggard; consider her ways, and be wise:"
Proverbs 6:6

Pride

Pride is the only trait included in both lists of the Seven Deadly Sins and the Abominations to God. The word 'pride,' a derivative of proud, may carry some beneficial attributes such as a proper sense of self-value *(positive self-esteem)* and a justifiable satisfaction of acts of goodness. However, it can also easily fall into negative traits of human behavior. In general, 'pride' as determined in the Abominations to God and the Seven Deadly Sins is a self-imposed excessive proportion of self-esteem synonymous to:

haughtiness
superior birth and or position
arrogance
self-importance displayed by treating others
with contempt or disregard

conceitedness
unjustified opinions of self qualities and abilities

As you can see, pride is an act of over-confidence in self. It is an unjustified feeling of being superior to others and being overly pleased with self and self-accomplishments. In the book of Ecclesiastes, written by King Solomon (son of King David), pride is negative in every sense of the word. It is often considered the sin from which all sins arise. King Solomon calls it vanity. Here are a couple of scriptures written about pride called vanity.

"vanity of vanities, all is vanity."
Ecclesiastes 1:2

"I have seen all the works that are done under the sun; and, behold, all is vanity and vexation of spirit."
Ecclesiastes 1:14

Pride is putting self before and above the reverence of God. In the 10 Commandments of God, you will find the inclusion of these words.

"Thou shall have no other gods before me."
Exodus 20:3

God is a jealous God, and there is no one or nothing higher than He is. You are encouraged not to think more highly of yourself than you ought. In the book of Romans, Paul states,

"For I say, through the grace given unto me, to every man that is among you, not to think of himself more highly than he ought to think; but to think soberly, according as God hath dealt to every man the measure of faith."
Romans 12:3

Pride at its very essence is a violation of the commandments of God. To have other gods before God, our Heavenly Father, may be subtle or it may be clearly evident. A subtle example may be to dedicate one's entire life to being good and doing good deeds without any acknow-ledgment of God. A more evident pattern of pride in one's life may be to worship a god or other gods while repudiating The True and Living God and His Son, as do many religions in our world today. Both examples indicate a life outside the will of God. They are hindrances to being in the presence of God at His Throne of Grace. Pride is the ultimate lack of obedience to God. It is a form of complete selfishness.

The infiltration of pride in one's life, regardless of the situation, tends to imply that the creature (man) is acting as if he is greater than the Creator (God, our Father). It is also implied that God is not needed in one's life. A prideful person in word and/or works self-boasts in a myriad of deeds and actions. His actions may be obvious or obscure. Nevertheless, one thing is sure; he tends not to acknowledge God through Jesus Christ as the source of his strength and achievements. Let it be known that the power behind all good things is produced by the power of God.

In both Old and New Testament, pride is clearly identified as a negative trait. Here are a few examples in verse:

"When pride cometh, then cometh shame: but with the lowly is wisdom."
Proverbs 11:2

"Only by pride cometh contention: but with the well advised is wisdom. Wealth gotten by vanity (pride) shall be diminished: but he that gathereth by labour shall increase."
Proverbs 13:10-11

"In the mouth of the foolish is a rod of pride: but the lips of the wise shall preserve them."
Proverbs 14:3

"Pride goeth before destruction and a haughty spirit before a fall."
Proverbs 16:18

"A man's pride shall bring him low; but honour shall uphold the humble in spirit."
Proverbs 29:23

"For from within, out of the heart of men, proceed evil thoughts, adulteries, fornications, mur-

ders, thefts, covetousness, wickedness, deceit, lasciviousness, an evil eye, blasphemy, <u>pride</u>, foolishness: <u>All these evil things come from within, and defile the man.</u>"
Mark 7:21-23

"For all that is in the world, the lust of the flesh, and the lust of the eyes, and the pride of life, is not of the Father, but is of the world."
1ˢᵗ John 2:16

If you are inclined to possess the deadly sin and abomination to God identified as pride, you may demonstrate acts of superiority and arrogance in your daily life. These behaviors may also manifest themselves in countercultures such as the Aryan Nation, the Black Panthers and others. Pride rears its ugly head among different denominations of congregations. It is institutionalized within our social and economic class structure, such as:

1) the dignity of the 'haves' and   stigma of the 'have nots'
2) the intellectually privileged and the disadvantaged illiterate

If you think about it, you can find pride in every walk of life. Prideful people cannot find themselves in the presence of God at His Throne of Grace because they think they are too good and righteous all by themselves. They cannot be in the presence of God at His Throne of Grace because they think they are higher than God is. They think they are god in their own field, or even worse, they may think there is no God. The Bible says,

"The fool hath said in his heart, There is no God".
Psalm 14:1a

All who are too proud to acknowledge, thank and praise God for their life, health, strength and energy hinder prayer with carnal minded behaviors. Carnal minded behaviors are works of the flesh and not the spirit.

"So then they that are in the flesh cannot please God."
Romans 8:8

All activities of life without God are vain (prideful) and useless. Should you detect pride in your life and want to communicate with God in His presence at His Throne of Grace, as a way of life, here is a simple prayer for you.

"Turn away mine eyes from beholding vanity;
and quicken Thou me in Thy way."
Psalm 119:37

King Solomon concludes his observations by saying,

"Let us hear the conclusion of the whole matter: Fear God, and <u>keep His Commandments: for this</u>

is the whole duty of man. For God shall bring every work into judgment, with every secret thing, whether it be good or whether it be evil."
Ecclesiastes 12:13-14

Envy

Envy is an unquenchable antagonism concerning someone else's joys, pleasures, and benefits. It is a lack of self-satisfaction because of the willful desire to want what someone else has. It is the resentful, begrudging feeling of wanting another's possessions; be it real or imagined. Envy blinds the eyes of reality, poisons the godly soul and repels the presence of God in one's life. It is an extremely dangerous trait, closely related to jealousy and covetousness. The actions of these kindred spirits are often (but not always) directed from a personal standpoint to someone in their familiar surroundings. Compare the 10th of the Ten Commandments with this deadly sin and abomination to God. Review covetousness in chapter four of this book.

The Bible says envy and strife *(usually derived from anger)* are brothers of destruction.

"For where envying and strife is, there is confusion and every evil work."
James 3:16

"For wrath killeth the foolish man, and envy slayeth the silly one."
Job 5:2

It seems that our world of "**I wanna, but...**," is fertile ground for the fiendish acts and ungodly behaviors of envy. Examples:

I want a good job, but I do not want to work. Therefore, I am envious of anyone in my surroundings that has a job and seem to be doing all the things I want to do. I want their joy but I do not want to do what it takes to have that joy.

I want to have a formal education, but I do not want to study.
I am envious of anyone in school, studying and achieving the goals I want to achieve. I want to achieve, but I do not want to do what it takes to achieve.

I want to have money, but I do not want to save money.
 I am envious of those around me who have saved their money and spent their savings on themselves for things I would like to have. I want to purchase material things to my heart's desire, but I do not want to give up any immediate gratifications for long-term goal accomplishments.

I want to lose weight, but I do not want to exercise and diet.
I loathe friends and family members who have changed their lifestyle for the better by losing weight and maintaining a healthy diet. I want to be trim and healthy, but I do not want to change my eating habits or my physical activity in order to accomplish this goal.

These attitudes stretch wide and deep into our culture today. They frequently go beyond our immediate surroundings and extend to the world at large. They frequently graduate into crime, national and international conflict. Envy and its associates, jealousy, greed, covetousness and anger hinder prayers that come before the Throne of Grace in the presence of God.

In this **"I wanna but..."** world, wants are greater than needs and true needs are seldom wanted. Envy, lust and covetousness caused the decision of the sons of Jacob to sell Joseph to the Ishmaelites. Envy caused the Philistines to cut the hair of Sampson. Envy and lust caused David to have Uriah the Hittite killed in battle. Down through the ages, when sin prevails, envy along with its comrades jealousy, greed, and covetousness is more than likely in the mix. If you have acknowledged envy in your life, and want to make a change be encouraged. Here are some scriptures just for you.

"Let not thine heart envy sinners: but be thou in the fear of the Lord all the day long."
Proverbs 23:17

"Let us walk honestly, as in the day; not in rioting and drunkenness, not in chambering and wantonness, not in strife and envying."
Romans 13:13

"Envyings, murders, drunkenness, revelings, and such like: of the which I tell you before, as I have also told you in time past, that they which do such things shall not inherit the kingdom of God."
Galatians 5:21

God is able and stands ready to change your ways. Do you believe this? If so, ask God to help you give up envious ways. He can and He will do all things above all that you may think. Pray to remove envy from your life as you enter His presence, at His Throne of Grace and it *(envy)* will flee from you.

Anger

On one hand, anger is the act of being irritated, enraged, resentful, or filled with wrath. It is a sense of great annoyance that by thought, expression or action catapults into sin. On the other hand, anger that creates feeling of great displeasure, hostility, indignation or exasperation because of the acts of sin is not sin. It is a strong sensitivity against sin. The Bible says,

"Be ye angry, and sin not: let not the sun go down upon your wrath:"
Ephesians 4:26

In the Gospel recorded according to Matthew, Jesus says,

"But I say unto you, that whosoever is angry with his brother without a cause shall be in danger of the judgment:"
Matthew 5:22a

"Moreover if thy brother shall trespass against thee, go and tell him his fault between thee and him alone: if he shall hear thee, thou hast gained thy brother."
Matthew 18:15

Anger that is not propelled by sin is often called righteous indignation. One example of righteous indignation illustrated in the Bible is the incident of merchants in the temple selling their merchandise while also exchanging money. When Jesus saw this, He was enraged.

"And Jesus went into the temple of God, and cast out all them that sold and bought in the temple, and overthrew the tables of the moneychangers, and the seats of them that sold doves, And said unto them, It is written, My house shall be called

the house of prayer; but ye have made it a den of thieves."
Matthew 21:12-13

Jesus was indeed angry, but He did not sin. His actions were brought on by the willful disrespect that merchants and moneychangers had for God's House, the House of Prayer. The Bible has several verses concerning this subject.

"He that is slow to anger is better than the mighty; . . ."
Proverbs 16:32a

"Cease from anger, and forsake wrath: fret not thyself in any wise to do evil."
Psalm 37:8

"For His (God's) anger endureth but a moment;"
Psalm 30:5a

Even though there may be times in this life where justification of righteous anger is warranted, the Bible encourages you not to rush into wrathful or anger-provoking situations. Be slow to anger and make every attempt in all states of affairs to live in peaceful harmony.

"The Lord is merciful and gracious, slow to anger, and plenteous in mercy."
Psalm 103:8

"If it be possible, as much as lieth in you, live peaceably with all men"
Romans 12:18.

Have righteous indignation about acts of sin, but do not let the sun go down on your anger. Should you find yourself in the midst of righteous indignation, hold fast to the guidance of the Holy Spirit. Present yourself in His presence, at His Throne of Grace in supplication, petition and intercession as needed for His goodness and mercy concerning each situation.

Greed

When I have more than I need, I give to rid myself of greed. There are many people less fortunate than I am. The once greed stained windows of my eyes can now see. My heart now opens to share the blessings given to me. Jesus gave His life not for me alone but for everyone to be free. God has met my every need and has washed my soul of all my greed.
Curtis Evans

Greed is an overwhelming wicked desire to gain more than is needed. Greed and gluttony are very similar. A glutton is greedy primarily for physical things, especially food. The greedy are gluttons for material things, especially wealth. Both words are frequently interchanged in today's vernacular. Greed and gluttony tend to ignore the spiritual principles of life. Instead, they incessantly seek unrestrained selfish worldly desires.

Like gluttony, greed is also associated with covetousness. Covetousness usually involves an irresistible desire to have what someone else has. While greed consists of the same emotion, it tends not to be as personal as covetousness. Covetous people tend to seek what someone else has whether it brings wealth or not. Greedy people seek abundance and wealth on almost any term.

Some kind hearted when shopping may buy just a little more to share with the poor. The very rich when shopping want to buy the whole grocery store. But as for me, God is my sustainer, He gives me my daily bread. In Him, I am well fed.
Curtis Evans

Greed starts in the heart and, if left un-checked, it develops into all manners of sins. It thrives on false assumptions.
Ex:
1) By obtaining all I want, I shall be happy.
   Greed can neither buy nor bring happiness.
2) If I am wealthy, I can have all I want
   Wealth cannot buy Salvation.

"And He spake a parable unto them, saying, The ground of a certain rich man brought forth

plentifully: And he thought within himself, saying, What shall I do, because I have no room where to bestow my fruits? And he said, This will I do: I will pull down my barns, and build greater; and there will I bestow all my fruits and my goods. And I will say to my soul, Soul, thou hast much goods laid up for many years; take thine ease, eat, drink, and be merry. But God said unto him, Thou fool, this night thy soul shall be required of thee: then whose shall those things be, which thou hast provided? So is he that layeth up treasure for himself, and is not rich toward God."
Luke 12:16-21

False witness and pride can be close associates of greed.

"The getting of treasures (greedily) by a lying tongue is a vanity (pride) tossed to and fro of them that seek death."
Proverbs 21:6

Greed and its associates are wicked habits to avoid. They are deadly sins of which to repent. It must be stated that all people of wealth are neither greedy nor covetous. It may also be noted that there are impoverished individuals who demonstrate the characteristics of greed and covetousness. The Bible says,

"Be ye angry, and sin not: let not the sun go down upon your wrath: Neither give place to the devil. "He that is greedy of gain troubleth his own house;"
Proverbs 15:27a

"For their feet run to evil, and make haste to shed blood..., So are the ways of every one that is greed of gain; which taketh away the life of the owners hereof."
Proverbs 1:16, 19

The Seven Deadly Sins as they relate to prayer hindrances have now been explained in brief. Never forget that the major objective of sin is to kill all opportunities for man to live in eternity with Christ, the Savior of us all. Contained in the words that follow are the abominations, repugnant behaviors of man that God loathes. Many of these abominations are also very similar to the Ten Commandments. They were detailed in chapter four of this book.

Lying tongue

Lying tongues, false witness that speaks lies and false witness against thy neighbor are all similar in nature. They exemplify the exact opposite of God and His attributes of truth and righteousness.

"God is not a man, that he should lie; (IN ANY SENSE OF THE WORD) neither the son of man,

that he should repent: hath He said, and shall He not do it? or hath He spoken, and shall He not make it good?"
Numbers 23:19

All forms of lies are of the devil. The devil is the exact opposite of God. God will not lie. God cannot lie. God is truth and His word is Truth.

"Thy word is truth."
John 17:17b

"let God be true"
Romans 3:4b

The devil is a liar and the father of all lies. All lies and liars are an abomination to God.

"Ye are of your father the devil, and the lusts of your father ye will do. He was a murderer from the beginning, and abode not in the truth, because there is no truth in him (the devil, satan). When he speaketh a lie, he speaketh of his own: for he is a liar, and the father of it."
John 8:44

Acts of deceit, fraud, and intentionally misleading gossip, half-truths, ingratiating facts, omitting details, slander, flattery and the like are all forms of a lying tongue. Lying under oath is considered the primary form of false witness. Speaking untruths about those of whom one is in close contact on a regular basis such as the family, the community, the workplace, and the church are all included in the term false witness against your neighbor.

Lying tongues are often found among gossipers and talebearers. Lying under oath, lying about friends and neighbors or just simply lying about anything are all abominations to God. Each of them carries a severe consequence.

"A false witness shall perish:"
Proverbs 21:28a

"There is no such thing as white lies; all lies are as dark as mud and can get just as dirty.
Curtis Evans

"Thou shall not bear false witness against thy neighbor", is included in the Ten Commandments. To bear false witness and to wag a lying tongue are in direct disobedience to God. King Solomon identifies false witness in this way:

"A man that beareth false witness against his neighbour is a maul, and a sword, and a sharp arrow."
Proverbs 25:18

A maul is a heavy, long-handled hammer used for pounding or beating. A sword (a long knife) is an instrument designed to pierce and sever with the intent to kill at close range. A sharp arrow *(a sharp pointed projectile with a slender shaft)* is shot from a bow with the same intent as the sword but from a distance. Each of the three devices listed in Proverbs 25:18 is used as a weapon designed to maim and to kill. Therefore, the above verse could be translated as follows:

A man that tells lies on his neighbor is the same as a hammer, a long knife, or a sharp missile used to attack with the intent to kill.

Surely, one does not expect to come in the presence of God at His Throne of Grace when identified as the above. Lying tongues and false witness can be murderous. Avoid them at all costs.

"A false witness shall not be unpunished, and he that speaketh lies shall not escape."
Proverbs 19:5

God cannot tolerate sin. All lies are sin. So, should you find yourself exercising a lying tongue or bearing false witness, please note the word of God on this issue.

"And be renewed in the spirit of your mind; And that ye put on the new man, which after God is created in righteousness and true holiness. Wherefore putting away lying, speak every man truth with his neighbour: for we are members one of another."
Ephesians 4:23-25

It is clear to see that all forms of lying can easily be hindrances when in the presence of God at His Throne of Grace.

Shedding innocent blood

Deaths caused by catastrophe and natural disaster are not thought to be shedding innocent blood. Deaths caused during acts of war are not usually called the shedding of innocent blood. Death caused by mechanical malfunction may not fall into the category of the shedding of innocent blood.

Shedding of innocent blood is a willful act of violence that causes death, whether premeditated or unplanned. For example:

1) A thief who unexpectedly kills to obtain what is not his is one who sheds blood of the innocent.

2) A practical joker *(a mischievous person)* whose prank causes death may be said to shed blood of the innocent.

3) A drunk driver who causes an automobile accident resulting in death is said to shed innocent blood.

4) Gang members whose drive-by shootings cause the death of an innocent bystander shed innocent blood.

Although not specifically intentional, the four examples above may indeed be included in the principle of shedding of innocent blood. Isaiah in chapter 59 verses 1 through 7 explains that activities such as the ones mentioned lead to a path of destruction. Here is verse 7 of Isaiah 59.

"Their feet run to evil, and they make haste to shed innocent blood their thoughts are thoughts of iniquity; wasting and destruction are in their paths."

The preceding examples of shedding of innocent blood exemplify violations of the sixth commandment of God mentioned in chapter 4. They are violations of God's rule for social order. Those who shed innocent blood are guilty of the wrath of God. The Bible states that a murderer or one who sheds innocent blood should surely be put to death.

"He that smiteth a man, so that he dies, shall be surely put to death."
Exodus 21:12

"And if he smites him with an instrument of iron, so that he die, he is a murderer: the murderer shall surely be put to death. And if he smite him with throwing a stone, wherewith he may die, and he die, he is a murderer: the murderer shall surely be put to death. Or if he smite him with

an hand weapon of wood, wherewith he may die, and he die, he is a murderer: the murderer shall surely be put to death."
Numbers 35:16-18

Excluding war, regardless of how or with what, when an act of intentional murder is done it is a sin deemed worthy of the penalty of death. The willful shedding of innocent blood is an abomination to God. Offenders will not go unpunished. Murders will not go unpunished. Do not get involved with the shedding of innocent blood.

On the other hand, Christians should be mindful of **THE INNOCENT BLOOD** forever and always. This **Innocent Blood** can take away the sins of the world. This **Innocent Blood** makes it possible for all sinners to be purged from the penalty of death and damnation. This **Innocent Blood** can keep sinners from total separation from God. This **Innocent Blood** is **THE BLOOD OF JESUS**, the unblemished Lamb of God who died but rose again so sinners may be saved from eternal damnation.

"...Behold the Lamb of God, which taketh away the sin of the world."
John 1:29b

Jesus, the Son of God, is the **Innocent Blood** of which Judas betrayed.

118

"Then Judas, which had betrayed Him (Jesus), when he saw that he was condemned, repented himself, and brought again the thirty pieces of silver to the chief priests and elders, Saying, I have sinned in that <u>I have betrayed The Innocent Blood</u>."
Matthew 27:3-4

In both the Old Testament and the New Testament, it is made quite clear that there can be no atonement (reparation) for sin without the shedding of blood.

"And almost all things are by the law purged with blood; and without shedding of blood is no remission."
Hebrews 9:22

Old Testament believers in God were allowed to atone for their sins by offering a blood sacrifice, the blood of clean unblemished animals such as lambs, doves, etc.

"And Noah builded an altar unto the Lord; and took of every clean beast, and of every clean fowl, and offered burnt offerings on the altar."
 Genesis 8:20

"And the Lord smelled a sweet savour; and the Lord said in His heart, I will not again curse the ground any more for man's sake;.."
Genesis 8:21

However, at this time, there is no remission of sin without the shed blood of Jesus. Jesus is the Lamb of God. He has fulfilled the laws of animal blood sacrifices.

"Think not that I am come to destroy the law, or the prophets: I am not come to destroy, but to fulfil."
Matthew 5:17

He is the final and ultimate sacrifice for the sins of man.

"...we shall be saved by his life. ...For if by one man's offence death reigned by one; much more they which receive abundance of grace and of the gift of righteousness shall reign in life by one, Jesus Christ."
Romans 5:10c, 17

By His blood, all mankind may be redeemed. It is because of the self-sacrifice of Jesus that we can be forgiven of our sins including murder. It is because of Jesus, that we can come boldly to the Throne of Grace in the presence of God to communicate with Him. *(Read the entirety of Romans chapter 5)*All believers are given the privilege to pray because Jesus, became human flesh, was born of a virgin, dwelled among us on earth, was crucified, died, was buried, resurrected and ascended into heaven for all believers. Had He not done this, there would be no forgiveness of sins, no hope, and no eternal life in the place that He is preparing for all believers right now.

"...I (Jesus) go to prepare a place for you.
And if I go and prepare a place for you, I will come again, and receive you unto myself; that where I am, there ye may be also."
John 14:2b-3

Our Lord and Savior Jesus Christ went through this suffering, this anguish and agony for all mankind. He shed His Innocent Blood for every believer. It is because of Him that each believer may have an opportunity to be forgiven of all sins. If you believe that Jesus is the Son of the **Most High Living God** with all your mind, body and soul, you have the right to eternal life.

"For God so loved the world, that He gave His only begotten Son, that whosoever believeth in Him should not perish, but have everlasting life. For God sent not His Son into the world to condemn the world; but that the world through Him (His Son) might be saved."
John 3:16-17

Upon the return of Jesus, believers will be with Him in the new heaven and new earth. For whoever has shed innocent blood, killed or murdered with full knowledge, malice and intent, can be forgiven by **The Innocent Blood** of Jesus. Those who shed innocent blood have an opportunity to be forgiven of all trespasses great and small alike. Sin is sin and all believers must be forgiven of all their sins. God, through Jesus Christ, His Son, can forgive every one of all sins.

All you have to do is believe that Jesus is the Son of God. Confess and repent of your sins. Submit to Him. Be His disciple. Then you will have no trouble coming to the Throne of Grace in the presence of God as a way of life, because Jesus Christ is the Innocent Blood that takes away the sin of the world. Be forgiven of your sins, even the shedding of innocent blood. Accept the Innocent Blood of Jesus, The Christ. He is the perfect Lamb, the atonement for your sins. Jesus is the Son of the Living God, our Father in Heaven. All believers will dwell with Him when He returns.

"And I saw a new heaven and a new earth: for the first heaven and the first earth were passed away; and there was no more sea. And I John saw the holy city, new Jerusalem, coming down from God out of heaven, prepared as a bride adorned for her husband. And I heard a great voice out of heaven saying, Behold, the tabernacle of God is with men, and he will dwell

with them, and they shall be his people, and God himself shall be with them, and be their God. Revelation 21:1-3

Wicked Imaginations

Did you know that sin is usually initiated through one's imagination? The more we imagine things outside the will of God, the more likely we set ourselves up for sin. Sin is both an inward state of being and an outward conduct of life that transgresses the laws of God. This means that sin can be a thought. It can be an action. It also can be a combination of both thought and action. Wicked imaginations are indeed sin. They interfere with prayer in the presence of God at His Throne of Grace as a way of life.

Wicked imaginations generate all kinds of deadly sins. They are truly an abomination to God. Wicked imaginations tend to be pro-gresssive. They anchor in the core of man's soul. They shackle truth and impede God's word. They stand firm in all aspects of immorality on a daily basis.

"He (the wicked) sitteth in the lurking places of the villages; in the secret places doth he murder the innocent; his eyes are privily set against the poor."
Psalm 10:8

123

"...and sin, when it is finished, bringeth forth death."
James 1:15b

Wicked imaginations tend to follow the same progression as lust. Wicked imaginations are capable of being covert and overt realities. The result of them always leads to death and eternal damnation.

Psalm 1:1 of the Old Testament is used to illustrate the progression of wicked imaginations. It is divided into three stages of progression:

1) **_Blessed is the man that walketh not in the counsel of the ungodly,_**   **_verse 1a_**

For whatever reason, wicked imaginations usually spring up from ungodly situations and circumstances in life. First, they are in an upright, slow-paced position _(the man that walketh in the counsel of ungodliness)_. This first action may be considered the pondering, the brooding or contemplative stage of wicked imaginations. It is a passing thought, a blurred image, a brief saunter or stroll around the seat of the scornful. This is the initial image of sin.

2) **_nor standeth in the way of sinners,_**

                                verse 1b

The second stage, still upright but with less mobility, _(standeth in the way of the sinful)_ a little more than a passing thought; it is an act of lingering. It hangs around and loiters in the mind. It is no longer a vague impression or a passing fancy. It is the focusing stage, headed straight for the seat of transgression. This stage, as the first, is unpleasing to God. It is a position of danger if you expect to enter the presence of God at His Throne of Grace in prayer as a way of life. In this stage, the imagery is more substantial. It can be called the preparation period; the time deliberately with premeditation set for establishing unrighteous goals and objectives.

3) ***nor sitteth in the seat of the scornful.***

verse1c

The third and final stage of wicked imaginations is no longer a passing thought, a lingering impression or preparation period. It is now sedentary *(sitteth in the seat of scornfulness)*. This stage is a full-fledged and completely contemptuous sin in total disobedience to the righteousness and will of God. It is an action or thought destined to defile and condemn its thinker. More often than not, those interned in prison will painfully admit that their actions were premeditated. They took time to think about how they would commit their wrong doings *(walked)*. Then they lingered, associated with sinners or continued to think of sinful acts *(stood).* Finally they sat in the seat of the scornful *(committed the act)*. At this point, they have become the devil's catch. Many caught in the snares of Satan wish over and over again that they had never continued in the wicked imaginations that led them to incarceration. They wished they had known and understood the verse that follow:

"But those things which proceed out of the mouth come forth from the heart; and they defile the man. For out of the heart proceed evil thoughts, murders, adulteries, fornications, thefts, false witness, blasphemies: These are the things which defile a man:"
Matthew 15:18-20a

Wicked imaginations are true hindrances to prayer in the presence of God at His Throne of Grace. But, Glory to God! You can overcome this abomination of wicked imaginations. The **Innocent Blood**, of Jesus Christ has made it possible for you to receive God's blessings. You can do this by confessing, and repenting of sins with a contrite heart and a right spirit. God is not a God that He should lie. He is able to forgive and to cleanse from all unrighteousness.

When wicked imaginations approach, and indeed they will, rush to the presence of God at His Throne of Grace. Ask God to remove wicked thoughts and imaginations from infiltrating your mind. Pray that your thoughts do not become actions. Pray that God create a clean heart and right spirit within you.

"Purge me with hyssop, and I shall be clean: wash me, and I shall be whiter than snow. Make me to hear joy and gladness; that the bones which thou hast broken may rejoice. Hide thy face from my sins, and blot out all mine iniquities. Create in me a clean heart, O God; and renew a right spirit within me."
Psalm 51:7-10

Mischief

Mischief stems from an underlying source of lighthearted harm and mild but annoying irritations. It is often guised as a childish misbehavior. Therefore, it frequently, goes without correction. It includes practical jokes, pranks, shenanigans, monkeyshines, teasing, and all sorts of unnecessary jesting. These activities can be attributed to immaturity at any age. They are seldom disapproved or corrected.

Is there such a thing as lighthearted harm, or mild irritations of devilishness that need no correction? The very definition of mischievousness leads to the impression that manifestations from actions of this word stem strictly from the devil. In the Bible, Job 15:35 points out that when mischief is conceived, it brings forth vanity, *(pride),* and the belly of them who conceive it prepare for deceit, *(dishonesty)*. All dishonesty is unrighteousness. All unrighteousness is sin. All mischief is sinful. Psalm 7:14 puts it this way:

"Behold, he travaileth with iniquity, and hath conceived mischief, and brought forth falsehood."

Mischief brings forth falsehood. Falsehoods are lies.

"...he (the devil) is a liar, and the father of it."
John 8:44g

Mischief is devilish and a favored tool in the devil's workshop. No matter how immature it may seem, mischief is sin and comes from the devil himself. Mischief has no place in the presence of God. It should never be considered the way for a Christ centered life.

Nevertheless, in our society we make light of mischief. Have you ever heard the phrase, *"Boys will be boys,"* or *"mischievousness is the spice of life?"* These terms are usually word fillers that emit thoughts of insignificant naughtiness. Sometimes they are heard as blank clichés. And even worse, they are given no thought at all.

What if you hear the following? Boys will be devils. Or, after all evilness and damnation is the spice of life. Would you be so casual when hearing these words? How would you feel if you knowingly had vile little devils in your home, school, community, country, and world; or if your own aspirations in life stemmed from mischief as now explained?

In fact, we do have devils in our every walk of life. All too often, we treat them as insignificant and harmless. Often we laugh at them. At times, we even consider their mis-behavior cute. When we do this, we fall right into the devil's trap. One day that cute little impish boy or girl will become a grown man or woman filled with all the characteristics of which he or she has been accustomed to as a child. If you are a parent, remember this scripture:

"Train up a child in the way he should go: and when he is old, he will not depart from it."
Proverbs 22:6

Start training each child as early as possible the way of God. Practice His way and teach your children to practice His way, so that they may not fall into the traps of the evil one.

"And ye shall teach them your children, speaking of them when thou sittest in thine house, and when thou walkest by the way, when thou liest down, and when thou risest up. And thou shalt write them upon the door posts of

thine house, and upon thy gates: That your days may be multiplied, and the days of your children, in the land which the Lord sware unto your fathers to give them, as the days of heaven upon the earth."
Deuteronomy 11:19-21

If you are not a parent, just keep this verse in mind:

"In all thy ways acknowledge Him, and He shall direct thy paths. Be not wise in thine own eyes: fear the Lord, and depart from evil. It shall be health to thy navel, and marrow to thy bones."
Proverbs 3:6-8

As stated earlier, the devil is a liar and the father of lies. Lies are deceitful. They make every effort to conceal and hide the truth. Yes, mischief is a dirty trick of the devil. In fact, it is one of his favorite tools used for the development of a sinful life in the heart of man. At an early age, little childish impish acts begin to block communication with God. Do not be fooled by seemingly innocent or insignificant acts of naughtiness in children as well as adults. Stop them immediately. They are not funny. They are tricks of the father of lies. He uses them to keep us from being in the presence of God at His Throne of Grace with a sincere and clean heart. Avoid practical joking, silly pranks, and all sorts of shenanigans. Do not allow presumably harmless acts of mischief to go unchecked.

Mischief is an abomination to God. It hinders prayer. It hampers a positive relationship with God. It may even sow discord among friends, and brethren. Should you find mischief in your life, swiftly approach the Throne of Grace in the presence of God and implore Him to help you overcome such acts. He is able to help you overcome mischief.

God is able to do exceeding abundantly above all that we ask or think, according to the power that works in us.
Ephesians 3:20

Let us have the power
to truly want to be within the will of God
rather than caught in the wiles of the evil one.
Take a godly stand against mischief.
Curtis Evans

Discord among brethren

This is the final abomination mentioned in the 6th chapter of the Book of Proverbs. The phrase simply means God hates troublemakers. Troublemakers are those who cause disagreement, strife, conflict and friction among two or more people in any given group. Wherever there are two or more people, the potential for discord among brethren is present, including the church. Do not be alarmed, but know this. Every Christian, disciple of Jesus Christ, has a cross to bear. The cross is sacrifice of self for the purpose of following and imitating Jesus even to death.

"...Whosoever will come after me, let him deny himself, and take up his cross, and follow Me. (Jesus)"
Mark 8:34b

When in the midst of discord among brethren may the words of this old song be of comfort to you.

> *Must Jesus bear the Cross alone*
> *and all the world go free?*
> *No, there's a cross for everyone.*
> *And there's a cross for me.*
> *The consecrated cross I'll bear,*
> *till death shall set me free,*
> *and then go home my crown to wear*
> *for there is a crown for me*
> Thomas Shepherd, 1665-1739

"I am crucified with Christ: nevertheless I live; yet not I, but Christ liveth in me: and the life which I now live in the flesh I live by the faith of the Son of God, who loved me, and gave Himself for me."
Galatians 2:20

From time to time, Christians may find themselves in discord among the nonbelievers and the
carnal minded. Fret not. Jesus is triumphant over
the evil that causes discord among brethren. By
His power, you may also be triumphant over
discord among brethren.

Nonbelievers and carnal minded people
may exhibit behaviors of troublemakers. They
are exemplified by tale bearing, gossip and any
form of perceived or unperceived causation of
discord. They love to spread rumors and tell
untruths. Troublemakers are those who have an
uncanny knack for telling just enough truth to
make their tale interesting and believable. Once
the venom of sharing distorted information has
spread, the result of such prattle is hurtful and
counter-productive. Troublemakers are thorns
and thistles in the vineyard of service to God.
They are irritating and if left unchecked may
cause much distress in any social group,
especially congregants of God. They can literally
rip up a congregation. Many a church has split
in half because of troublemakers or sowers of
discord among brethren. But know this; idle
words of a troublemaker will not go without
judgment.

"But I (Jesus) say unto you, That every idle word
that men shall speak, they shall give account
thereof in the day of judgment. For by Thy words

thou shalt be justified, and by thy words thou shalt be condemned."
Matthew 12:36-37

Pray heavily to prevent, *"A false witness that speaketh lies, and he that soweth discord among brethren"(Proverbs 6:19)*

"The words of a talebearer are as wounds, and they go down into the innermost parts of the belly."
Proverbs 18:8

In the book of Matthew, chapter 18, Jesus Christ provides a means for resolving discord among brethren in a specific manner.

"...if thy brother shall trespass against thee, go and tell him his fault between thee and him alone: if he shall hear thee, thou hast gained thy brother. But if he will not hear thee, then take with thee one or two more, that in the mouth of two or three witnesses every word may be established. And if he shall neglect to hear them, tell it unto the church: but if he neglect to hear the church, let him be unto thee as an heathen man and a publican."
Matthew 18:15-17

These verses provide a four-step process for overcoming conflicts caused by troublemakers in a Christian congregation.

1) *"...if thy brother shall trespass against thee, go and tell him his fault between thee and him alone: if he shall hear thee, thou hast gained thy brother."*　　　　*v.15*

The one who causes discord should be approached by the aggrieved. The aggrieved must explain the difficulty that has arisen. If the two can work it out, then each one has gained a brother and the discord has been settled.

2) *"But if he will not hear thee, then take with thee one or two more, that in the mouth of two or three witnesses every word may be established."*　　　　*v.16*

If the one who caused the discord refuses to attempt to work the discord out, then the offended one gets witnesses to approach the one who has caused the problem in order to help create a settlement. If the talebearer and the aggrieved individual can work it out in the presence of at least one or two witnesses, then the matter is settled.

3) *"And if he shall neglect to hear them, tell it unto the church:"*　　　　*v.17a*

If the troublemaker neglects to help resolve the matter before the witnesses; then process continues to the congregation of the church. If reconciliation is made at the congregation level, the brethren are reconciled. If reconciliation at this level is not achievable, the fourth and final step must be enacted.

4) *"but if he neglect to hear the church let him be unto thee as an heathen man and a publican.* *v.17b*

If no reconciliation is achieved, the one who is guilty of the discord should be treated as a non-Christian. There should be no fellowship with this individual until repentance occurs. This final process for curtailing discord may seem drastic. However, we must remember that God finds discord among the brethren abominable. This process, developed by Jesus the Son of God, is a strong deterrent for those who would sow discord among the brethren. No true Christian wants to be treated as a heathen *(one who is unconverted/one who does not acknowledge the will of God)* and a publican *(a tax collector/ held in the lowest esteem and placed in the same category as harlots)*. It seems reasonable that the troublemaker or the one who sows discord would rather repent than be ostracized in such a manner.

Discord among the brethren in the church must be corrected as soon as possible. Otherwise, it festers and will deteriorate and diminish the entire congregation. When allowed to fester, discord among brethren hinders prayers in the presence of God at His Throne of Grace.

Should you find yourself in the middle of discord among the brethren, think, **"WHAT WOULD JESUS DO?"** He would do exactly what He encourages you to do in Matthew 18:15-17. God forbid if the producer of discord is you. Mend your ways. No matter how interesting the information within your grasp may be, do not pass it on. If for some reason, you cannot resist, pray in the presence of God at His Throne of Grace for forgiveness and courage not to yield to temptation.

"Let us therefore come boldly unto the throne of grace, that we may obtain mercy, and find grace to help in time of need."
Hebrews 4:16

Be receptive to the aggrieved should he come to you. Ask for forgiveness. Encourage prayer with and for one another so that both of you may overcome behaviors of discord among brethren.

Keep praying in the presence of God
at His Throne of Grace, as a way of life.
God though His son, Jesus,
will not fail you.

A Prayer of Petition for Renewed Mind and the Love of God

My Father God in Heaven, purge me with hyssop, and I shall be clean. Renew my mind. Bless me to love You with all my heart, and with all my soul, and with all my mind. Let me delight in Your ways. Give me a mind of humility and a readiness to exercise Your will for me. You are my strength and my redeemer. You are my high tower and my fortress. My hope is in you. Let all iniquity pass from me. Keep me from all temptations and deliver me from all evil. Let the words of my mouth and the meditation of my heart be acceptable in Your sight. Let my attitudes and my motives be in accordance with Your Perfect Will. Let nothing keep me from communicating with You. For You are the Kingdom and the Power and the Glory forever, in the name of Jesus,
Amen.

Chapter 6
<u>Answers to Prayer</u>

*"And thine ears shall hear a word
behind thee, saying, This is the
way, walk ye in it, when ye
turn to the right hand, and
when ye turn to the left."*
Isaiah 30:21

Just as Jesus Christ, God's only begotten Son, taught His disciples a specific model prayer, there are specific ways in which God answers prayer. God answers all Spirit inspired prayers in His good time and for His good purpose. When we pray within the will of God without wavering, God does answer prayer in the way He wants not always in the way we want.

"For My thoughts are not your thoughts, neither are your ways my ways, saith the Lord. For as the heavens are higher than the earth, so are my ways higher than your ways, and my thoughts than your thoughts."
Isaiah 55:8-9

God's ways are far beyond the thoughts of man, nevertheless, He responds to prayer in ways understood by man, the pray(er).

Although God is not restricted to the descriptions explained in this book, He frequently responds to prayers within three categories. They are yes, no and wait. The examples given are but a tiny view in the window of answered prayer found in the Bible.

Yes

When you receive an answer of "yes" from our God in heaven, your prayer is within His will for you and for the good of all those involved in your concerns to Him.

1)   Elias prayed and God stayed the rain.

"Elias was a man subject to like passions as we are and he prayed earnestly that it might not rain: and it rained not on the earth by the space of three years and six months. And he prayed again, and the heaven gave rain, and the earth brought forth her fruit."
James 5:17-18

2)   During the prophecy of Elisha, Naaman the leper was healed, but only if specific directions were followed.

"Now Naaman, captain of the host of the king of Syria, was a leper.....So Naaman came with his horses and with his chariot, and stood at the door of the house of Elisha. And Elisha sent a messenger unto him, saying, Go and wash in Jordan seven times, and thy flesh shall come

again to thee, and thou shalt be clean. ...Behold, I (Naaman) thought, He will surely come out to me, and stand, and call on the name of the Lord his God, and strike his hand over the place, and recover the leper....Then went he (Naaman) down, and dipped himself seven times in Jordan, according to the saying of the man of God: and his flesh came again like unto the flesh of a little child, and he was clean.....Behold, now I know that there is no God in all the earth, but in Israel:"
2nd Kings 5:1, 9-11, 14, 15

Naaman went to the man of God, Elisha, with the expectation of some marvelous, miraculous actions concerning his healing of leprosy. God's instructions were simple. Go wash in the Jordan River seven times and you will be healed. Finally, Naaman did as he was told. God's word is true. Naaman was healed of his diseases. *Read the entire chapter of 2nd Kings chapter 5 for a clear picture of this account.* God answers prayer in His own time, in His own will, in His own way.

3)   Before there were kings in Israel, judges were chosen by God to deliver His people from their enemies. Samson, an impulsive, head-strong Nazarite *(one vowed to be dedicated to God for a special service)* from the tribe of Dan, was such a person chosen by God. Samson seemed to have

had little or no regard for his calling. *Judges, chapter 13 through 16 gives a full account of his actions.* Regardless of his behaviors, Samson acknowledged God. He did pray. He had a relationship with God. At the end of his life on earth, God answered 'yes' to Samson's final request. Samson was allowed to use his God given power to destroy the enemies of Israel. The will of God will always prevail. Samson was indeed a Nazarite of God.

"And Samson called unto the Lord, and said, O Lord God, remember me, I pray thee, and strengthen me, I pray thee, only this once, O God, that I may be at once avenged of the Philistines for my two eyes. And Samson took hold of the two middle pillars upon which the house stood, and on which it was borne up, of the one with his right hand, and of the other with his left. And Samson said, Let me die with the Philistines. And he bowed himself with all his might; and the house fell upon the lords, and upon all the people that were therein. So the dead which he slew at his death were more than they which he slew in his life."
Judges 16:28-30

God always answers prayer according to His will, His way, His purpose and for His Glory. When prayers are within His will, He always answers in ways that fit into His Perfect Will and

Devine Plan. Who would have ever thought that Samson would be able to devastate the Philistines in such a way as he did?

No

God's responses are always within His will. They are always for His glory, even if the answer is 'no.'

1)   Jesus prayed a prayer knowing that the mission before Him had to be completed. Nevertheless, He prayed, if possible to let the experience of the cross be taken from Him.

"And he went a little farther, and fell on his face, and prayed, saying, O my Father, if it be possible, let this cup pass from me: ...O my Father, if this cup may not pass away from me, except I drink it, thy will be done... And he left them, and went away again, and prayed the third time, saying the same words."
Read Matthew 26:39a, 42b, 44

In God's plan for humankind, there can be no remission of sin without the shedding of blood. This is God's plan and He will not change it.

Jesus suffered the cross and shed His **Innocent Blood** so that we may be redeemed to God. Without the mission of Jesus on the cross, there would be no hope for our Salvation. God the Father had to say 'no' to God the Son just for us. Can you imagine! God, the Creator of the

Universe sending His only begotten Son, to die for a bunch of selfish, hardheaded, disrespectful and ungrateful people? God did it. What a great and marvelous God we serve! He loves us so much that He gave Jesus, the Christ, to shed His **Innocent Blood** for us through the agony of the cross.

2) In anger, Jonah asked to die.

"...O Lord, take, I beseech thee, my life from me;"
Jonah 4:3b

Even when God says no, our Father in heaven remains compassionate.

"And the Lord God prepared a gourd, and made it to come up over Jonah, that it might be a shadow over his head, to deliver him from his grief. So, Jonah was exceeding glad of the gourd."
Jonah 4:6

Read the entire book of Jonah, chapters 1 through 4 for a full account of the occurrence. It truly exemplifies the love of God for all His people.

3) In the eighth chapter of Luke, Jesus heals a man possessed of several demons. Out of gratitude, the healed man asked to go with Jesus.

"Now the man out of whom the devils were

departed besought Him that he might be with Him: but Jesus sent him away...,"
Luke 8:38

God's answer through His Son, Jesus was no to the man who had been demon possessed. Read Luke, chapter 8 verses 28 through 40 to find out why. God's will supersedes all desires of man. God's will is always best not only for the immediate recipient of blessings, but also for others involved. Sometimes, it is just good to be around true believers in God.

4)   Paul prayed to God for the removal of a thorn in his flesh.

"there was given to me a thorn in the flesh, the messenger of Satan to buffet me, lest I should be exalted above measure.   For this thing I besought the Lord thrice, that it might depart from me.   And He said unto me, my grace is sufficient for thee: for my strength is made perfect in weakness. Most gladly therefore will I rather glory in my infirmities, that the power of Christ may rest upon me. Therefore, I take pleasure in infirmities, in reproaches, in necessities, in persecutions, in distresses for Christ's sake: for when I am weak, then am I strong"
2nd Corinthians 12: 7b-10

After making his request known unto God three times, Paul received his answer. *"My grace is sufficient for you,"* said the Lord. This response was not the initial desire of Paul, nevertheless, Paul submitted to God's answer wholeheartedly as indicated above in verse 10 of 2nd Corinthians chapter 12.

Wait

From time to time, a prayer of petition or intercession within God's will is made. However, it may not be within God's time frame to answer when requested. Waiting for His response and divine intervention may be necessary. God's delays in responding to prayers are not necessarily denials. Generally, the postponements may cause growth in faith and dependence on God in heaven when waiting is necessary.

1) Daniel prayed and waited patiently for an answer

"Then said he unto me, Fear not, Daniel: for from the first day that thou didst set thine heart to understand, and to chasten thyself before thy God, <u>thy words were heard, and I am come for thy words.</u> But the prince of the kingdom of Persia withstood me one and twenty days: but, lo, Michael, one of the chief princes, came to help me; and I remained there with the kings of

Persia. Now I am come to make thee understand what shall befall thy people in the latter days: for yet the vision is for many days."
Daniel 10:12-14

2)   In the 11th chapter of the Gospel of John, John records the conversation of Jesus with the sisters of Lazarus, His friend. The request for help concerning the illness of Lazarus by Mary and Martha was postponed for at least four days. During that time Lazarus died. In His own time and in His own way, Jesus, the Son of God, raised Lazarus from the dead. The request for healing was granted, but for God's will and purpose Lazarus had to die first. Drastic isn't it. God's ways are not our ways.

Read John 11:1-44 for the complete account.

Answered prayer *(communication with God)* parted the Red Sea establishing a path of dry land for the Israelites to escape from Egypt. Answered prayer gave a barren woman (Hannah) a child (Samuel) who was raised up to be a judge for God. Answered prayer caused fire not to burn the three Hebrew boys, (Shadrach, Meshach and Abednego) who had been thrown into a fiery furnace. Answered prayer locked the mouth of a lion and allowed Daniel to be safe in its den. Answered prayer healed the sick and raised the dead. Answered prayer made the lame man walk, the blind man see, the speechless man talk

147

and the leper cleansed. Answered prayer has done all this and even more. Answered prayer has delivered believers from sin and an everlasting hell. Answered prayer is the work and will of God. Answered prayer is a connection between God and man. Answered prayer glorifies God and benefits man. Answered prayer sends us to sleep at night and awakes us in the morning. Answered prayer is constant and ongoing. Answered prayer is the keeper of our souls. Answered prayer is an awesome event because God is an awesome God. Answered prayer is a reason to praise and thank God continually. Answered prayer should never be taken lightly. Answered prayer is a means of forming a strong and mature relationship with God.

"...call upon me, and ye shall go and pray unto me, and I will hearken unto you."
Jeremiah 29:12

Chapter 7
The Model Prayer

"I cried unto him with my mouth,
and he was extolled with my tongue.
If I regard iniquity in my heart,
the Lord will not hear me:
But verily God hath heard me;
he hath attended to the voice of my prayer.
Blessed be God, which hath not turned away my
prayer, nor his mercy from me."
Psalm 66:17-20

Jesus Christ is the Model Pray(er).

"And it came to pass, that, as He was praying in
a certain place, when He ceased, one of His
disciples said unto Him, Lord, teach us to pray,
as John also taught his disciples."
Luke 11:1

Jesus did not hesitate to instruct His disciples how to pray. The instructions He gave are found in the Gospel according to **Matthew 6:5-13** and according to **Luke 11:1-4.** It is important to note that the instructions for prayer were not only given by words but also demonstrated in the lifestyle of Jesus Himself. Jesus taught His disciples how to pray and He prayed often to His Father and our God.

To learn the language of prayer is to learn how to openly communicate with God. This leads to the development of a spiritually mature Christian lifestyle
Curtis Evans

When praying, address "Our Father" as Jesus instructed. Know that,

"...The Lord our God is one Lord:"
Mark: 12:29b

At the time of prayer, the entire Holy Trinity is attentive to what is prayed. The Holy Trinity is God, His undivided unity expressed in His threefold nature.

1) God the Father:
   The Creator of the Universe and all that dwells therein, the Godhead, of the Holy Trinity

2) God the Son:
   The expressed image of God; the Messiah, the Christ, the Savior and Lord of all believers The Son of the Godhead;

"And Jesus, when He was baptized, went up straightway out of the water: and, lo, the heavens were opened unto Him, and He saw the Spirit of God descending like a dove, and lighting upon Him: And lo a voice from heaven,

150

saying, *This is My beloved Son, in whom I am well pleased."*
Matthew 3:16-17

3) <u>God the Holy Spirit</u>:
   The essence of the Holy Trinity that dwells in the heart of all Christians. The Spirit of the Godhead

"I indeed baptize you with water unto repentance: but he that cometh after me is mightier than I, whose shoes I am not worthy to bear: he shall baptize you with the Holy Ghost, and with fire:"
Matthew 3:12

"If ye love me, keep my commandments. And I will pray the Father, and he shall give you another Comforter, that he may abide with you forever;"
John 14:15-16

The threefold unity of our Triune God *(God the Father, God the Son and God the Holy Spirit)* hears you when you pray. As you pray, you should automatically surrender to the Holy Spirit, who lives within you, a believer. He, The Holy Spirit, moves you to pray and guides your thoughts and words.

"...for we know not what we should pray for as we ought: but the Spirit itself maketh interces-

sion for us with groanings which cannot be uttered."
Romans 8:26b

Pray to God in the name of Jesus, who forever lives and makes intercession for you.

"... It is Christ that died, yea rather, that is risen again, who is even at the right hand of God, who also maketh intercession for us."
Romans 8:34b

Most prayers are in the form of submission, adorations, petitions, confessions, intercessions or any combination thereof.   Prayers in the presence of God at His Throne of Grace are under the guidance of The Holy Spirit, in the name of Jesus. *THE MODEL PRAYER* for all disciples of Jesus, frequently referred to as *THE LORD'S PRAYER*, is a model that God the Son has provided for communicating with God the Father. Jesus, God the Son of God gives specific directives concerning prayer.

"And when thou prayest, thou shalt not be as the hypocrites are: for they love to pray standing in the synagogues and in the corners of the streets, that they may be seen of men. Verily I say unto you, they have their reward. But thou, when thou prayest, enter into thy closet, and when thou hast shut thy door, pray to thy Father which is in secret; and thy Father which seeth in secret shall

reward thee openly. But when ye pray, use not vain repetitions, as the heathen do: for they think that they shall be heard for their much speaking. Be not ye therefore like unto them: for your Father knoweth what things ye have need of, before ye ask Him."
Matthews 6:5-8

Prayers **are not** directed toward men. Never pray to God for man's entertainment or amusement. Neither let prayer be a soapbox to express your own philosophy on a variety of issues. Nor should prayer be a platform for the exercising of prideful eloquence, or the ability to use rhythmic, repetitious words. Prayers are to be directed to God from the depths of the heart in simplistic sincerity. In return, God already knows what is needed even before asked. He will respond according to His will for His purpose and His glory.

"And whatsoever we ask, we receive of him, because we keep his commandments, and do those things that are pleasing in his sight. And this is his commandment, That we should believe on the name of his Son Jesus Christ, and love one another, as he gave us commandment. And he that keepeth his commandments dwelleth in him, and he in him. And hereby we know that he

abideth in us, by the Spirit which he hath given us."
1ˢᵗ John 3:22-24

"And this is the confidence that we have in him, that, if we ask any thing according to his will, He heareth us: And if we know that he hear us, whatsoever we ask, we know that we have the petitions that we desired of him."
1st John 5:14-15

The aforementioned scriptures from the Holy Bible are the conditions by which prayer is answered. The four statements below are prerequisites for positive communication with God and answered prayer.

1)   keep His commandments
     (review chapter 4 of this book)
2)   do what is pleasing in God's sight
     (review chapter 5 of this book)
3)   believe on the name of Jesus Christ,
     God's Son
     (a must for all believers) (see 1ˢᵗ John 3:22-24)
4)   love one another
     (a commandment of Jesus Christ)

"This is my commandment, That ye love one another, as I have loved you."
John 15:12

It is upon these principles that Jesus taught His disciples to pray.

The prayer that Jesus taught may be divided into at least seven divisions or focal prayer points:

1) Pray in the Name of the Father with reverence, and respect.

"Our Father which art in heaven, hallowed be Thy name,"

2) Pray expecting the kingdom of God to reign in the life of all believers.

"Thy kingdom come,"

3) Pray acknowledging and accepting the fact that God is Sovereign and He reigns on earth and in Heaven.

"Thy will be done in earth, as it is in heaven,"

4) Pray with confidence that God will provide.

"Give us this day our daily bread,"

5) Pray to forgive and to be forgiven.

"And forgive us our debts, as we forgive our debtors,"

6) Pray for protection and deliverance.

"And lead us not into temptation, but deliver us from evil:"

7) Pray edifying and praising God for all He is, at all times.

"for Thine is the kingdom, and the power, and the glory, forever. Amen"

It is unnecessary to use any other points of prayer when communicating with God. This model prayer covers it all. From time to time one focal point may be stressed more than another as the Holy Spirit leads when praying. Nevertheless, when put together, they are all inclusive.

Each division or focal point is discussed in detail as follows:

"After this manner therefore pray ye:"
Matthew 6:9a

Matthew 6:9b and c
<u>"Our Father which art in heaven, Hallowed be Thy name."</u>
Prayers of Adoration, Reverence, and Respect to our heavenly Father, the Godhead of the Holy Trinity

The first division in the Model Prayer for disciples is subdivided into three areas:

1)   to whom should you pray

God is our Father, the Lord God Almighty. We are His sons and daughters. If we accept Him through His Son, Jesus Christ, He will receive us.

"I (The Lord Almighty) will receive you. And will be a Father unto you, and ye shall be my sons and daughters, saith the Lord Almighty."
2nd Corinthians 6:17c-18

"One God, and Father of all, who is above all, and through all, and in you all."
Ephesians 4:6

As stated earlier, God, "Our Father", the God-head of the Holy Trinity is the One to whom we direct our prayers.

2)   where God resides

Our Father, God, the Creator of the Universe says He is in the heavens. Heaven is His throne and He rules over all.

"...But our God is in the heavens:"
Psalm 115:3a

"Thus saith the Lord, The heaven is my throne, and the earth is my footstool"
Isaiah 66:1a

"The Lord hath prepared His throne in the heavens; and his kingdom ruleth over all."
Psalm 103:19

Pray to God, our Father who resides in heaven.

3)   sanctify His name

When praying to God, "Our Father," in heaven we should hallow His name. To hallow His name means to hold His name with the highest regard, admiration and respect. "Our Father," God in heaven is Holy. None other is higher than He is. Honor Him with all reverence.

"Exalt the Lord our God, and worship at His holy hill; for the Lord our God is Holy."
Psalm 99:9

We pray to our Father, God in heaven in consecrated, sanctified holiness. We pray with the highest esteem, reverence and respect to God our Father, in heaven.

"For I am the Lord your God: ye shall therefore sanctify yourselves, and ye shall be holy; for I am holy:..."
Leviticus 11:44a

Because it is written, Be ye holy; for I am holy."
1ˢᵗ Peter 1:16

The God we pray to is **OUR FATHER**. He is the Father of Abraham, Isaac and Jacob. He is the Father of Moses and the Hebrew children. He is the Father of Daniel in the lion's den and the Father of Shadrach, Meshach and Abednego in the fiery furnace. He is the Father of our Lord and Savior Jesus Christ. Our Father, God in heaven, Creator of the Universe is the King of kings and Lord of lords. He is your Father and my Father. He resides in heaven. Direct your prayers to Him. Praise, revere, respect and adore Him. Hallow His name. Words of these well-known hymns come to mind when praying this portion of the Lord's Prayer.

Holy, holy, holy! Lord God Almighty!

Early in the morning our song (prayers) shall
rise to Thee; Holy, holy, holy, merciful and
mighty! God in Three Persons, blessed Trinity!
Reginald Heber, 1783-1826

To God be the glory,
great things He hasth done!
So loved He the world that He gave us His Son,
Who yielded His life an atonement for sin
And opened the life gate that all may go in
Praise the Lord! Praise the Lord!
Let the earth hear His voice!
Praise the Lord! Praise the Lord!
Let the people rejoice! O come to the Father
thro' Jesus the Son, And give Him the glory,
great things He hath done.
Fanny J. Crosby, 1820-1915

"Bless the Lord, O my soul: and all that is
within me, bless His holy name."
Psalm 103:1

Just to amplify what has been said, God, our Father in heaven, the one and only Holy God, the Godhead of the Holy Trinity is the Father of:
1) Adam and Eve in the Garden of Eden
2) Noah who survived the great flood
3) Job who lost everything but would not give God up
4) Joshua who defeated the Gibeons when God made the sun and moon stand still

5) Deborah, a female who lead Israel to victory

6) David who played the harp, killed the giant Goliath, ate the showbread, committed adultery, repented of his sins, and prayed to remain the apple of God's eye

7) Jonah who lived in the belly of a great fish for three days, before he did the will of God

8) Zacharias who became dumb until the day of birth of his son, John the Baptist, the forerunner of Jesus

9) Our Lord and Savior, Jesus Christ, God's only begotten Son

10) All who accept His only begotten Son as our Lord, and Savior

God our Father in heaven is the One and only true God with a threefold-undivided nature called the Holy Trinity or the Triune God. He is holy. He is to be revered and His name hallowed. Come before His presence at His Throne of Grace with all reverence and respect, knowing that God is in heaven. Surely, He will receive you at His Throne of Grace and bless you.

Matthew 6:10a
"Thy Kingdom Come."
Prayers of Submission, and Petition with Supplication for the Kingdom of God to reign

The first thing a believer must remember when praying this portion of our Lord's Prayer is,

"My help (the believer's help) cometh from the Lord, which made heaven and earth".
Psalm 121:2

In this division of the model prayer of Jesus to His disciples are four subdivisions. At least two scriptures in the Bible confirm these divisions.

"For the kingdom of God is not meat and drink; but righteousness, and peace, and joy in the Holy Ghost."
Romans 14:17

"For the kingdom of God is not in word, but in power."
1ˢᵗ Corinthians 4:20

These verses indicate God's kingdom is not identified in concrete terms, vastness of land, material riches, or worldly prestige. Instead, the kingdom of God is explained in terms of three abstract realities all within His and only His almighty power. They are righteousness, peace, and joy in the Holy Ghost.

Righteousness:

God's righteousness is ever lasting. It never changes.

"His work is honourable and glorious: and His righteousness endureth forever."
Psalm 111:3

Our God is infallible. He is faithfully righteous. He never errs. His judgment is honest and true. God's kingdom is righteous. When you pray, put your hope in the righteousness of God through His Son.

My hope is built on nothing less
Than Jesus' blood and righteousness
I dare not trust the sweetest frame,
But wholly lean on Jesus' name
On Christ, the solid Rock, I stand
All other ground is sinking sand.
Edward Mote, 1797-1874

Peace:

In God our Father's kingdom, there is peace. Peace is God's comfort to each believer. It is the inner security, serenity, contentment and completeness in God for each Christian whose hopes in the Lord. Although indiscernible and incomprehensible to the world, it is clear to all who believe in God through His Son, that the peace God gives comes by means of reconciliation with God because of the shed blood of Jesus Christ.

"Peace I leave with you, my peace I give unto you: not as the world giveth, give I unto you. Let not your heart be troubled, neither let it be afraid. Ye have heard how I said unto you, I go away, and come again unto you. If ye loved me, ye would rejoice, because I said, I go unto the Father: for My Father is greater than I."
John 14:27-28

"Be careful for nothing; but in everything by prayer and supplication with thanksgiving let your requests be made known unto God. And the peace of God, which passeth all understanding, shall keep your hearts and minds through Christ Jesus."
Philippians 4:6-7

"And let the peace of God rule in your hearts, to the which also ye are called in one body; and be ye thankful. Let the word of Christ dwell in you richly in all wisdom; teaching and admonishing one another in psalms and hymns and spiritual songs, singing with grace in your hearts to the Lord. And whatsoever ye do in word or deed, do all in the name of the Lord Jesus, giving thanks to God and the Father by Him."
Colossians 3:15-17

God's peace is harmony in the spirit of every Christian. God's peace is contentment in whatsoever state, circumstance or situation of which one may find himself. God's peace in you is demonstrated by the words and actions of your daily life. All that a Christian does should be done in the name of our Lord Jesus, for the glory of God, in full knowledge and experience of His peace. As you give thanks to God our Father, praise and revere Him for the peace He gives to you.

Let the peace of God rule in your heart and be thankful to Him for all He has done, is doing and will do for you. Adhere to the word of Christ in your every walk of life. Share His word with one another. Encourage one another with words from the psalms, uplifting hymns and spiritual songs. Keep a melody of Jesus in your heart as you live the life He has planned for you day by day. By doing these things, you are guaranteed the peace of God.

When peace like a river, attendeth my way,
When sorrow like sea billows roll
Whatever my lot Thou hast taught me to say
It is well; it is well with my soul.
Horatio G. Spafford, 1826-1888

When praying, "Thy Kingdom Come", pray for the peace of God in your life. The peace of God that passes all understanding is available to you.

Joy in the Holy Ghost:

God's kingdom represents joy in the Holy Ghost. Pray that the pure joy in the Spirit come in your daily life. The Holy Spirit of God produces this joy. This joy looks beyond current circumstances and focuses on the glory of God.

"... neither be ye sorry; for the joy of the Lord is your strength."
Nehemiah 8:10c

"If ye keep my commandments, ye shall abide in my love; even as I have kept My Father's commandments, and abide in His love. These things have I spoken unto you, that My joy might remain in you, and that your joy might be full. This is My commandment, That ye love one another, as I have loved you."
John 15:10-12

The joy of the Lord is strength. The joy of the Lord remains in all who keep the commandments of Jesus. This is especially evident in the commandment, **'*love one another*'** as Jesus has loved us. The love He has for you is abundant and cannot be exceeded.

"Greater love hath no man than this that a man lay down his life for his friends. Ye are my friends, if ye do whatsoever I command you."
John 15:13-14

How marvelous and what great joy is our God! He gave His Son who stated the words you just read. Greater love hath no man than The One who gave His life for His friends. If you do whatever He commands, you are His friend. Doers of His word are His disciples. They are Christians.

"And the disciples were called Christians first in Antioch."
Acts 11:26c

There is great joy in the Spirit *(in the Holy Ghost)* for every Christian.

"But let all those that put their trust in thee rejoice: let them ever shout for joy, because thou defendest them: let them also that love thy name be joyful in thee."
Psalm 5:11

All Christians are friends of Jesus, the Son of the living God. What great joy!

Needless to say, the source of the joy of which we speak does not come from family, friends or significant others. It is found in the Holy Ghost, the Comforter, by means of Jesus, the only begotten Son of God. Joy in the Spirit comes through the love of Jesus. Greater love hath no man than Jesus for us. If you ever find yourself, lonely, weary or sad the joy in the Holy Ghost is available for you. Take it. Be strengthened by joy in the Spirit of our Triune God.

The joy of the Lord is invigorating. The joy of the Lord is energizing. The joy of the Lord is the stimulus that encourages the willing soul to do the work of God for His glory. The abiding love of Jesus gives this joy. If you love one another as He has loved you, you will have joy in the Holy Ghost. Keep His commandment to love one another. Pray that your love for another be contagious. Pray that the joy in the Spirit of God in you be transmitted to all you encounter.

By praying, "Thy Kingdom Come" you are asking for God's joy. You are asking for His joy to strengthen you in times of frustration and distress. When your closest friends, family, coworkers etc. let you down and it seems that no one cares, God cares. He loves you. He is your joy. When persecution for the sake of Christ is all around and it seems as if everyone is gone, God is there. He loves you. His Son calls you friend. When your heart aches and it seems as if no one can ease your pain, God can. He loves you. He is your joy. The joy of the Lord is your strength. He can give you peace in the midst of any trial. He can give you joy during turmoil and sorrow. Trust Him. Try Him. Let His kingdom come in your life. Take the joy that only God through Jesus Christ can give. Pray for the kingdom of God to come in your life. In it is righteousness, peace, and joy in the Holy Ghost by the power of God.

Power:

In the kingdom of God, there is power. When you pray for God's kingdom to come, you are praying for the power of God's authority to reign in your life. When you submit to the righteous authority of God in your life, He can give you power for His glory.

"Behold, I give unto you power (authority) to tread on serpents and scorpions, and over all the power of the enemy: and nothing shall by any means hurt you."
Luke 10:19

This portion of prayer should not be taken for granted. It represents the power of the Almighty Triune God who guides you through each day. When you submit to the kingdom of God, you may be endowed with His strength and power, His joy, His peace and His righteousness.

God's kingdom is power, not words only. His power is manifested by His Word. Believers are privileged to exercise His power in daily living for His glory. Genesis, chapter one, shows the power of God's word concerning everything that was made. **"And God said...."** He just spoke the word and the world was made. Glory to God! What a powerful God we have.

O Lord my God, when I in awesome wonder
consider all the world Thy hands have made.
I see the stars. I hear the rolling thunder,
Thy power throughout the universe displayed.
Then sings my soul, my Savior God, to Thee,
How great Thou art, How great Thou art.
Carl Gustav Boberg, 1885

Why not praise Him? Why not show respect to Him? Why not honor Him? Why not obey Him through His Son, Our Lord Jesus Christ? The source of all righteousness, peace, joy, and power come from God our Father through Jesus Christ, His Son and our Savior. It is by the mercy and grace of His power that we have our very being. Whatever we need is within His power to give. The breadth, and length, and depth, and height of all He is, is infinite. God is incalculably righteousness. He is indescribable peace. He is unspeakable joy in the Holy Ghost and He is unfathomable power.

Included in this section of prayer are petitions for God's kingdom to reign in the life of every pray(er). "Thy Kingdom Come" spoken in prayer declares an awesome concept. In fact, God through Jesus Christ promises to give each believer a Comforter, The Holy Spirit. He will abide with you always. "Thy Kingdom Come" represents righteousness, peace, joy in the

Holy Spirit and the action of His power and strength to everyone who believes. Accept this promise of God. Pray for His kingdom to come in your life.

Do not give up the opportunity to communicate with God in the splendor of His kingdom at His throne of Grace when you pray. Thy Kingdom Come is a powerful segment of prayer. Do not rush through it or take it lightly.

Matthew 6:10b
"Thy Will Be Done In Earth, As It Is In Heaven."
Prayers of Submission, Petition and Supplication

In this third segment of prayer, again you must acknowledge your submissiveness to our Holy Father, God in heaven. You must have confidence in the realization that His will is done here in earth as it is done in heaven. You may severely question this concept. How can a Hallowed and Holy God whose kingdom is righteousness, peace, joy in the Holy Ghost by the His sovereign power permit such devastating wickedness and destruction to occur on earth? Know this: God has a *Devine Plan* for all believers. This plan is nestled in *His Perfect Will*. As God would have it, man has volition, the right to make his own decisions. The decisions of man are found in *God's Permissive*

Will.   God's Perfect Will never changes.
Nevertheless, He permits man to use his own
will (make his own decisions) concerning The
Perfect Will of God. Many have chosen not to
follow the Perfect Will of God. Thus, chaos is
created. However, chaotic occurrences in earth
have not changed God's overall plan for
mankind. He remains faithful. ***His Perfect Will,***
will prevail.

　　　Those who have chosen God's will over
self-will (man's volition) are on a battlefield, at
spiritual war against principalities, powers, rulers
of the darkness of this world and spiritual
wickedness in high places.

"...we wrestle not against flesh and blood, but
against principalities, against powers, against
the rulers of the darkness of this world, against
spiritual wickedness in high places."
Ephesians 6:12
(This verse will be discussed later in the eighth chapter
of this book and briefly mentioned in segment six of this
chapter, „Lead us not into temptation, but deliver us from
evil.')

Believers in God, through His Son, struggle
against these forces. No matter how bad it
seems, no matter how the human volition is used,
God's Perfect Will cannot be shattered. Here are
three unfailing essentials that must manifest in
the life of a Christian no matter how brutal this

spiritual war may seem. The Christian must remain steadfast in his heart and behavior with assured confidence that God's will in earth as it is in heaven will prevail.

Essential one:
Believe in Jesus, the Son of God

"For God so loved the world that he gave his only begotten Son, that whosoever believeth in him should not perish, but have everlasting life."
John 3:16

Essential Two:
Once you believe, immediately ***Seek His Kingdom.*** Seek His righteousness. Seek His peace. Seek His joy in the Holy Ghost. Seek His power and authority for your life.

"But seek ye first the kingdom of God, and his righteousness; and all these things shall be added unto you."
Matthew 6:33

Essential Three:
Along with the acceptance of essentials 1 and 2 ***accept your body as a part of the temple of our Triune God.*** God dwells in you.

"Know you not that ye are the temple of God, and that the Spirit of God dwelleth in (lives in) you?"
1st Corinthians 3:16

If you believe in Jesus, seek to do His will and His way. His will and His way are righteousness, peace, and joy in the Holy Spirit by His power. If you let Him, He will dwell in you. Is it possible to live with someone and not communicate with that person? Take a sincere minute to answer this question.

"What? Know ye not that your body is the temple of the Holy Ghost which is in you, which ye have of God, and ye are not your own? For ye are bought with a price: therefore glorify God in your body, and in your spirit, which are God's."
1ˢᵗ Corinthians 6:19-20

Unceasing prayer is essential here. Pray the will of God in your life. Glorify Him in your body and spirit. That is, do your best for Him according to His will for you in every aspect of your daily living. Understand and live the following scriptures with a clean and contrite heart.

"...whatsoever things were written aforetime was written for our learning, that we through patience and comfort of the scriptures might have hope. Now the God of patience and consolation grant you to be likeminded one toward another according to Christ Jesus: That ye may with one mind and one mouth glorify

God, even the Father of our Lord Jesus Christ."
Romans 15:4-6

"...whatsoever things are true, whatsoever things are honest, whatsoever things are just, whatsoever things are pure, whatsoever things are lovely, whatsoever things are of good report; if there be any virtue, and if there be any praise, think on these things."
Philippians 4:8

In this section of prayer, pray that God's will be done in your life here on earth as His will is done in heaven.

Matthew 6:11
"Give us this day our daily bread."
Prayers of Petition-Supplication and Intercession

The fourth section of the Lord's Prayer, acknowledges God as provider of all needs and desires. Just as He did for the Hebrew children in the wilderness, God is able to provide our daily sustenance. *(Read Exodus 16:15-35)*For every believer in Christ, God is the source of hope for eternity. He is the provider of all physical, emotional and spiritual needs. It is by His will that we awake, eat, go through the necessities of the day, and retire in preparation for another day at night. All this is given freely according to His grace and mercy.

174

"Gracious is the Lord, and righteous; yea, our God is merciful."
Psalm 116:5

"...his merciful kindness is great toward us: and the truth of the Lord endureth forever. Praise ye the Lord.
Psalm 117:2

"The Lord is gracious, and full of compassion; slow to anger, and of great mercy."
Psalm 145:8

Growth and maturity in a relationship with Him requires that requests be made known unto Him. This may be done by the most obvious and simple to the most obscure and complex forms of communication granted to each believer. This section of prayer clearly indicates that communication with God should at the very least be on a daily basis. God knows our heart, our needs and our desires before we ask for them. Nevertheless, He wants continued communication with us.

"...for he knoweth the secrets of the heart."
Psalm 44:21b

"...your Father knoweth what things ye have need of, before ye ask him."
Matthew 6:8b

It is His requirement that we communicate with Him continually.

"Pray without ceasing."
1st Thessalonians 5:17

Petitioning, and interceding for others on a daily basis are the focal point in this section. It is important that thoughts and words explain exactly what daily needs and concerns are in our petitions. According to His will, He can and He will grant requests for us and our intercessions for others.

"And all things, whatsoever ye shall ask in prayer, believing, ye shall receive."
Matthew 21:22

As long as one believes in God through His Son, Jesus Christ and is determined to do His will, God is prepared to answer all prayers within His will in a way that is always best for the pray(er). Here are five things to remember when petitioning, supplicating and interceding in prayer:

1)   acknowledge God as your sufficiency,
2)   have confidence that God will answer
      your prayers,
3)   be specific with your requests,
4)   have patience while awaiting God's answer
      with full knowledge that His answer is
      best for you,

5) be submissive and accept God's answer to your prayer.

These five statements concerning your requests for God's provisions are conditions not only for this segment of prayer, but for all prayers rendered to God at His Throne of Grace in His presence, as a way of life. Please know that God will supply all your needs according to His will. You must accept His will for the requests you make. By doing so, you acknowledge and appreciate the fact that His determination for you is always better than your own imperfections and selfish resolves.

"...our sufficiency is of God;"
2ⁿᵈ Corinthians 3:5b

Never waver in the certainty that God will answer prayer according to His will. God always answers the prayers of a sincere unwavering heart according to His Devine plan and purpose. That is, your prayers of petition and intercession must be within His design and intentions for you as well as for those of which you pray. Confidence in Him and His way allows you to receive the desires of your heart. Because your desires are within His will, for His glory. You ask amiss when you do not make your petitions, and intercessions in accordance with His plan for you. ***NOT YOUR PLAN FOR***

YOU; BUT HIS PLAN FOR YOU. Pray with confidence in His will.

"But let him ask in faith, nothing wavering. For he that wavereth is like a wave of the sea driven with the wind and tossed. For let not that man think that he shall receive any thing of the Lord. James 1:6-7

The more specific you are in your requests for yourself and others, the more specific God's response to you will be. Your specificity and precision in asking for provisions makes it easier for you to see and understand the blessings of God when He answers you. Ask God specifically for what you want. He is the provider of all good things.

Be consistent, persistent and patient with your prayers. As long as they are within God's will, He will answer them. His answer will be in His own time frame. He knows what, when, where, why and how to provide His boundless blessings with an abundance of grace and mercy.

"...what man is there of you, whom if his son ask bread, will he give him a stone? Or if he asks a fish, will he give him a serpent? If ye then, being evil, know how to give good gifts unto your children, how much more shall your Father

which is in heaven give good things to them that ask Him?"
Matthew 7:9-11

When God answers your prayers, accept His answer. Remember He knows what is best for you. He is your sufficiency. He is your great provider. If you trust Him, if you submit to His will and way for you, He will direct your path in every endeavor.

"Trust in Him at all times; ye people, pour out your heart before him: God is a refuge for us.
Psalm 62:8

A word of caution: It has been said that many Christians, especially immature Christians tend to get stuck on this portion of prayer with much neglect of the six other focal points included in our Lord's model prayer. Their regular communication with God becomes one of, "Lord, give me this, and Lord, give me that." Do not be fooled. Our Lord is faithful and just. He knows what you want. He knows what you need. He knows your maturity level. He knows your heart. He knows what is best for you at all times. Never be reluctant to ask God for the sincere desires of your heart. Trust Him to determine what will sustain you for this day, this time, this season, all for His glory. Do not be discouraged if the answers to your prayers are not exactly what you desired. Neither be overly surprised if God's answers to your prayers are greater than you requested. Just trust God. He will provide.

As in all learning experiences, the more you practice, the better you get. Communication with God is no different. The more you pray the better pray(er) you become. Be determined to pray and to pray often. The will of God will be developed in your prayers as you learn more and more of Him. The give me prayers are OK if that is all you know at this time. Often in the beginning, you do not know how to accept the leading of the Holy Spirit in your prayers. Do not stop praying. With practice you will know when the Holy Spirit is leading and guiding you in prayer. Many give me prayers will be within the will of God and answered immediately. Many give me prayers will be within God's will but delayed for His own purpose. In this instance, it may just be that God wants to reveal to you how determined you really are for the fulfillment of the request you have made. Many give me prayers are not within God's will. God will not grant anything outside of His will. When God says no to give me prayers, He knows what is best for you. The overall concept in this portion of the model prayer is to trust God and submit to His will for all your needs. It may be important to note that God looks upon the following give me situations unfavorably. Most of which have been explained as hindrances to prayer detailed in chapter five of this book.

The slothful:
"...that if any would not work, neither should (he) eat."
2nd Thessalonians 3:10c

People who are not disabled, but refuse to work need not pray for things outside of their grasp due to their own laziness. God is not 'their servant' to adhere to their beckoning.

"He becometh poor that dealeth with a slack hand: but the hand of the diligent maketh rich."
Proverbs 10:4

"The soul of the sluggard desireth, and hath nothing: but the soul of the diligent shall be made fat."
Proverbs 13:4

"Seest thou a man diligent in his business? he shall stand before kings; he shall not stand before mean men."
Proverbs 22:29

"...do your own business, and to work with your own hands, as we commanded you;"
1st Thessalonians 4:11b

God is our heavenly Father. He knows our innermost being. He knows what we can and cannot do. He encourages His children to work.

The wasteful:

"He also that is slothful in his work is brother to him that is a great waster."
Proverbs 18:9

Those who initially have, but squander, waste and misuse God's blessings may one day find themselves without, as did the *Prodigal Son* spoken of in *Luke chapter 15.* It may be good for the sloth and the wasteful to be obedient to *1st Thessalonians 4:11* before they come into the presence of God at His Throne of Grace with a give me prayer.

The selfish:

"But whoso hath this world's good, and seeth his brother have need, and shutteth up his bowels of compassion from him, how dwelleth the love of God in him?"
1st John3:17

Selfish people are always seeking a personal advantage. They are individuals who care too much for themselves and too little for others. Selfish people may do well to adhere to the following verse.

"Be kindly affectioned one to another with brotherly love; in honour preferring one another; (not self alone, but one another)
Romans 12:10

The greedy:

"He that is greedy of gain troubleth his own house;"
Proverbs 15:27a

Greedy people may demonstrate attributes of all of the above. They are avaricious in their behavior. They always want more than they need.

"But my God shall supply all your need according to his riches in glory by Christ Jesus."
Philippians 4:19

These situations lead to the fact that God's will is not always the will of man. The overall function of prayer is to bring believers closer to God, His will and His way for them so that He may be glorified. It is by no means a way for man to encourage God to change His will for the specific benefits of any individual or group of people. God will never submit to the will of man and his selfish, lustful, evil ways. How can the created become the master of the Creator? It is you, His creation who must submit to Him, The Creator. His grace is sufficient for all your needs. Accept His will and His way for your daily bread. He is the true and faithful provider. Let your prayers be within His will. He answers prayers within His Devine and permissive will. He will supply your every need and desire within His will. As you mature in His grace and mercy, His will for your life will indeed become your will to glorify Him.

Matthew 6:12
"And Forgive Us Our Debts, As We Forgive Our Debtors."
Prayers of Confession, Supplication- Petition and Intercession

In this section of the Lord's Prayer, some pray(ers) fall short of being in the presence of God at His Throne of Grace as a way of life for at least three reasons. In the first example, genuineness is present but the prayer is erroneous. In example two, the level of genuineness in prayer tends to lack sincerity and contrition. The last example illuminated in this book is denial of a need to pray for forgiveness of self and/or others entirely.

1) **Erroneous Prayer:**

Sometimes sincere prayers for forgiveness are prayed and are forgiven. Yet, because of overwhelming emotional guilt, one makes the same request over and over again. If you have earnestly prayed with contrition for forgiveness

184

and have not repeated that same sin, know this.

"If we confess our sins, he is faithful and just to forgive us our sins, and to cleanse us from all unrighteousness."
1ˢᵗ John 1:9

"Come now, and let us reason together, saith the Lord: though your sins be as scarlet, they shall be as white as snow; though they be red like crimson, they shall be as wool."
Isaiah 1:18

When guilt of previously forgiven sins reoccur, instead of repeating prayers for sins already forgiven, praise God for forgiving you of that sin and then let it go. Every time it comes up praise God for His forgiveness and let it go. Pray to God to remove untrue guilty thoughts from your mind. Do so by praising God through His Son Jesus Christ with a mind-set on His faithfulness. Here is a helpful scripture verse for situations such as this.

"Lord, I believe (you have forgiven me for (say the specific sin)); help Thou mine unbelief."
Mark 9:24b

2) **Lack of genuineness in prayer:**
   Sometimes you pray knowing that you have not asked for forgiveness of those you have trespassed against nor have you forgiven others who have trespassed against you. You tend not to

talk to God about your need to be forgiven or your need to forgive others. These violations lurk in the deepest darkest depths of your heart.

You attempt to keep your unforgiveness a secret. Even worse than that, sometimes, you pretend forgiveness of others outwardly; but inwardly you have nothing but contempt and utter disrespect for the one who has trespassed against you. Be careful here. These hidden and suppressed negative emotions can cause phys-ical, psychological and spiritual trauma. Forgive and request forgiveness. Negligence in this area leads to no good. Hear these words.

"He that covereth his sins shall not prosper: but whoso confesseth and forsaketh them shall have mercy."
Proverbs 28:13

"If I regard iniquity in my heart, the Lord will not hear me:
Psalm 66:18

"Be not deceived; God is not mocked: for whatsoever a man soweth, that shall he also reap."
Galatians 6:7

Many a good man has caused even more heartache and more sin because he has not forgiven or sought forgiveness. If you have sinned, even if it is known only to yourself, you must forgive and ask forgiveness before coming to the presence of God at His Throne of Grace when you pray. Your sin may be secret to most men but it is never secret to God. So why are you attempting to hide your sins? Surely you have heard the old cliché, *"You can fool all of the people some of the time and you can fool some of the people all the of time; but you cannot fool all the people all of the time."* It is a true saying. The fact is, **"You cannot fool God at any time."** God is omnipotent, omnipresent and omniscient. He is all-powerful. He is present everywhere. He is all knowing. You cannot hide from Him. Nothing is too great or too small for Him to know. Nothing is too great or too small for Him to forgive. So tell Him all, even your deepest, darkest sinful secrets. He knows them anyway. He stands ready to forgive you as you forgive yourself and others.

"For if ye forgive men their trespasses, your heavenly Father will also forgive you: But if ye forgive not men their trespasses, neither will your Father forgive your trespasses."
Matthew 6:14-15

Forgive and ask for forgiveness. Ask God to,

"cleanse thou me from secret faults. Keep back thy servant also from presumptuous sins;"
Psalm 19:12b-13a

God can do this. "But it is hard to forgive others, especially when they sin against you over and over again," you say. I agree with you. Listen to the conversation between Peter and Jesus concerning this very matter.

"Then came Peter to him (Jesus), and said, Lord, how oft shall my brother sin against me, and I forgive him? till seven times? Jesus saith unto him, I say not unto thee, Until seven times: but, Until seventy times seven."
Matthew 18:21-22

This passage of scripture may seem difficult to put into action, but it is the will of God through His Son Jesus our Savior, that you forgive one another. Just think about it. How many times have you been forgiven? Yes, my brothers and sisters, you are encouraged by God to forgive one another over and over again.

"And be ye kind one to another, tender-hearted, forgiving one another, even as God for Christ's sake hath forgiven you."
Ephesians 4:32

Even so, you say, some sin is extremely hard to forgive. One example prevalent in our current day society is abuse. How can you keep on forgiving someone who abuses you on a regular basis? Yes, intentional and perpetual abuse is a hard thing to forgive. Nevertheless, know this.

188

All abuse is sin. Therefore, abuse must be forgiven. However, abuse and life threatening circumstances of this world has never been within the perfect will of God. Yes, you must forgive and be forgiven for acts involving abuse.

However, you must never allow yourself to be abused repeatedly under the guise that such behavior is within the will of God. Abuse is not and never will be within the perfect will of God.

Abuse comes in many forms; the most obvious are physical and emotional maltreatment. They may be classified into these three categories at least:

1) child abuse and neglect
2) elderly and parental abuse and neglect
3) spousal abuse and neglect

Not one of the preceding forms of abuse is acceptable behaviors to God. Look at what is said about the 5th commandment in chapter 4. Parental abuse is worthy of death. Now look at the followings scripture verses.

"Wives, submit yourselves unto your own husbands, __as it is fit in the Lord.__ Husbands, love your wives, and be not bitter against them. Children, obey your parents in all things: for this is well pleasing unto the Lord. Fathers, provoke not your children to anger, lest they be discouraged."
Colossians 3:18-21

A key phrase here is '***as it is fit in the Lord***.' It isn't fit in the Lord to be abused or to be abusive in any relationship, at any time, under any circumstance, never, not at all. Another key phrase is, 'provoke not your children to anger.' A child provoked is a discouraged child. Incessant discouragement is a form of psychological abuse.

Abuse of any kind must be turned over to the proper authorities immediately. Get out of abusive situations without delay, but do not sin. It is clear that within the laws and statutes of God that intentional bodily and/or emotional injury of any form is contrary to the will of God. If you are being abused, remove yourself from the abuser, report the abuse and pray that the abuser be delivered from that sin. If you are an abuser, remove your own-self from situations that cause you to abuse. Pray for the strength and courage to stop this wicked behavior. God is able. Just trust Him.

Our God through His Son, Jesus Christ is a forgiving God. He forgives repeatedly. You, His child, should have the same character. Be kind, tenderhearted and forgiving to each other. Do what our Lord would have you do. You will be blessed of Him mightily for your obedience to Him. He can give you the will and power to cease abusing self and others. Here are some words for those who are married.

Marriage
is that relation between man and woman
in which the independence is equal,
the dependence is mutual
and the obligation is reciprocal."
Louis K. Anspacher, 1934

The world may say no to this concept of forgiving and being forgiven. But our God and Father in Heaven says, 'yes'. To whom is your allegiance? Be genuine in your prayers. Genuineness when praying will automatically cultivate allegiance to God.

"And when ye stand praying, forgive, if ye have ought against any: that your Father also which is in heaven may forgive you your trespasses. But if ye do not forgive, neither will your Father which is in heaven forgive your trespasses."
Mark 11:25

3) **Denial of the need for forgiveness**

The third weakness in this area of prayer is a forgiveness needed but denied. Although sin is present, there is no feeling of need to repent. No remorse is felt. The sinner does not view trespasses against God or man as wrongdoings. This is an extremely dangerous state of being. The sinner is callus and hardened against the truth of God. Godly sorrow and the need for repentance are far from this sinner. This sinner in his self-righteous state has no serious desire to pray for forgiveness or to forgive others who have trespassed against him. This state leads to the following.

"And even as they did not like to retain God in their knowledge, God gave them over to a reprobate mind, to do those things which are not convenient; Being filled with all unright-eousness, fornication, wickedness, covetous-ness, maliciousness; full of envy, murder, debate, deceit, malignity; whisperers, Backbiters, haters of God, despiteful, proud, boasters, inventors of evil things, disobedient to parents, Without understanding, covenant breakers, without natural affection, implacable, unmerciful: Who knowing the judgment of God, that they which commit such things are worthy of death, not only do the same, but have pleasure in them that do them."
Romans 1:28-32

Praying in this state *(other than for confession of need to forgive and to be forgiven)* more than likely, may receive the answer No!

"Ye ask, and receive not, because ye ask amiss"
James 4:3

Because prayers are amiss, and the answer is no, one tends not to seek God's presence at

His Throne of Grace. He seldom prays. He totally ignores the will of God in his life. Often he takes on many of the negative characteristics mentioned in *Romans 1:28-32*. He gets further and further away from God's precepts and more distance from communication with God. Negative aspects of this state of mind lead to the continuance of disregard, disrespect and even disbelief in God. A person in this state denies any reason to believe God's truths. As a result, the relationship with God diminishes daily. If this pattern continues, he will cut off his relationship with God completely of his own volition.

"But unto them that are contentious, and do not obey the truth, but obey unrighteousness, indignation and wrath, tribulation and anguish, upon every soul of man that doeth evil, of the Jew first, and also of the Gentile; But glory, honour, and peace, to every man that worketh good, to the Jew first, and also to the Gentile: For there is no respect of persons with God."
Romans 2:8-11

Some scriptural words for pray(ers) when having difficulty forgiving and asking for forgiveness are listed below. Read them. Meditate on them. Act on them.

"Hide Thy face from my sins, and blot out all mine iniquities. Create in me a clean heart, O God; and renew a right spirit within me. Cast me not away from Thy presence; and take not Thy holy spirit from me. Restore unto me the joy of Thy salvation; and uphold me with Thy free spirit."
Psalm 51:9-12

"...cleanse Thou me from secret faults. Keep back Thy servant also from presumptuous sins; let them not have dominion over me: then shall I be upright, and I shall be innocent from the great transgression. Let the words of my mouth, and the meditation of my heart, be acceptable in Thy sight, O Lord, my strength, and my redeemer."
Psalm 19:12b-14

"Search me, O God, and know my heart: try me, and know my thoughts: And see if there be any wicked way in me, and lead me in the way everlasting."
Psalm 139: 23-24

Pray to forgive and to be forgiven by others. It may not be as hard as you may think. Read this verse below.

"...for we know not what we should pray for as we ought: but the Spirit itself maketh intercession for us with groanings which cannot be uttered. And He that searcheth the hearts

knoweth what is the mind of the Spirit, because He maketh intercession for the saints according to the will of God. And we know that all things work together for good to them that love God, to them who are the called according to His purpose."
Romans 8:26b-28

If you yield your all to God through His Son, the Holy Spirit will help you in your weaknesses. He will intercede for you when you do not know how to pray, as you should. If your heart is right, God will hear you by the groaning of the Holy Spirit. Pray in the presence of God at His Throne of Grace with a sincere and contrite heart. Pray to forgive. Also, pray to be forgiven for all sins. If you do not, a consequence is sure to come.

"But if ye forgive not men their trespasses, neither will your Father forgive your trespasses."
Matthew 6:15

Matthew 6:13a
"And Lead Us Not Into Temptation, but Deliver Us from Evil:"
Prayers of confession, petition-supplication, and intercession

Satan, the devil, just as he is the father of lies, is also the great tempter. It is he, the wicked one who entices, solicits, seduces, and provokes everyone he can to sin.   Do not be deceived. Satan is frequently successful in his mission. Therefore, Jesus in His loving kindness has left a directive, to overcome the devil's shrewd, wily, cunning and sin-provoking capers through the process of prayer. This segment of "The Lord's Prayer offers an opportunity to pray for guidance and protection. Put on The Whole Armor of God is a precept to use when seeking God's protection and guidance. The Whole Armor of God is a daily requirement for all situations and circumstances of life. It is completely necessary when seeking protection from the wiles of the evil one. It will be detailed in chapter eight of this book.

Temptation frequently comes to the fore-front in the form of things of which you are familiar.   Temptation is usually comfortable within your own human frailties and natural inclinations for sin. For example: If you do not drink alcoholic beverages, you most likely will never become an alcoholic. However, if you are comfortable with casual or social drinking, then there is a clear possibility that the evil one may entice you to drink more and more. Before you know what hits you, you will be dependent on liquor rather than God as your daily sufficiency. Everyone knows that alcoholic beverages cannot provide for your physical health. It cannot maintain emotional and financial security. Most importantly, it never stimulates spiritual growth. Nevertheless, the father of lies entices you to feel as if you cannot live without it *(although you may say to others, you can)*. At that point, over consumption of alcohol becomes your sin. Anything that takes the place of the will of God in your life is a sin. As the scripture below states, God is faithful. He will provide a means of escape from any temptation you may face. All you have to do is pray not to be led into temptation by the great tempter.

"There hath no temptation taken you but such as is common to man: but God is faithful, who will not suffer you to be tempted above that ye are able; but will with the temptation also make a way to escape, that ye may be able to bear it."
1ˢᵗ Corinthians 10:13

If the tempter should seduce you, our loving and compassionate Jesus has left this simple guideline to overcome the wiles of the devil. Ask for deliverance! It is in this section of the Lord's Prayer or Model Prayer that petitions with supplication to God to guard against the wiles of the evil one. Pray that you may know and understand how to use the Whole Armor of God to protect you from the ways of the world and the tricks of the devil. Pray to overcome the

197

tactics of the great seducer's deceit, false teachings, and false beliefs. It is his pleasure to lure you away from the will of God, our Father in Heaven.

The great seducer, Satan, encourages you to believe that your sinful condition is too entrenched for positive change or too insignificant for a need of changing. You have often heard this phrase repeated by lifers in prison, *"I ain't got nothing to lose."* Whether guilty or innocent of the initial cause of incarceration, inmates with an attitude such as that tend to sin over and over again. They deliberately relinquish all possibilities of freedom (physical and spiritual) because they feel they have reached rock bottom or a point of no return. They feel that there is no way to come up from and out of their miry clay. They are in a quagmire of hopelessness. The father of lies has duped them. They are just where he wants them to be. This perpetually false outlook on life results in a soul lost to eternal condemnation. Don't be deceived. The devil is a liar and the father of lies. He is a misleader and a deceiver. He is the great tempter. No matter what he may lead you to believe, the truth is, there is no situation or circumstance too great or too small for God's intervention.

When the concept of, *"I ain't got nothing to lose,"* is actualized, it is at this point that all can be gained from God. Just think about it. If you have nothing to lose, it would seem that there is nothing left but to gain. Try Jesus. Submit to Him, the Creator of all things. Confess your sins to Him. He answers prayer. God saves. God changes things for His glory and His perfect will. Is there any problem that God cannot solve? Is there any sin that God cannot forgive?

"Behold, the Lord's hand is not shortened, that it cannot save; neither his ear heavy that it cannot hear:"
Isaiah 59:1

The devil is delighted when man of his own will, determines a situation as impossible to remedy. Nevertheless, our God is glorified when in the midst of the impossible, man turns to Him. God can make the impossible possible. Remember, God deplores sin and will have no part of it. By His grace, compassion and mercy, He can and does forgive. You can go to God in prayer for anything within His will. It is His will to forgive sin. David prayed the prayer below. You can pray it also.

"The troubles of my heart are enlarged: O bring thou me out of my distresses. Look upon mine

affliction and my pain; and forgive all my sins."
Psalm 25:17-18

Seek to gain eternal life with the God who answers prayer.

Although it is possible, prayer may not always obliterate or completely erase your past sinful experiences from your mind, it can and does cause resistance from the actualizations of them again. For Example: you may never forget the fact that sleeping in bed with a lit cigarette caused the destruction by fire of your place of residence and perhaps the loss of a loved one. However, if you have sincerely heeded the consequence of sleeping in bed with a lit cigarette, nothing on earth can cause you to smoke in bed again. Likewise, for one confined in prison for life, *(if he has truly accepted the consequence of his behavior and is sincerely repentant)* perhaps, he may never be set free physically from prison because of the penalties of breaking the law. Nevertheless, there is a God in heaven who can set his soul free from the eternal curse of everlasting death caused by sin.

Prayer is the key that can set a soul free. It can unlock the door that separates man from communication with God. Prayer can cleanse a heart from worldly infestations to one infiltrated with joy in the Holy Ghost and power from on High. It can transform the mind from one of misery and despair to one of renewed attitudes of righteousness and peace. Come into His presence, at His Throne of Grace as a way of life. He is willing and able to deliver you beyond your wildest dreams. Do not allow the evil one to deceive you or seduce you with maneuvers that lead straight into sin and bondage.

"Blessed is the man that endureth temptation: for when he is tried, he shall receive the crown of life, which the Lord hath promised to them that love Him."
James 1:12

Yield not to temptation for yielding is sin. Each victory will help you some other to win. Fight manfully onward, dark passions subdue. Look ever to Jesus, He will carry you through. Ask the Savior to help you comfort, strengthen and keep you. He is willing to aid you. He will carry you through.
Haratio R. Palmer 1868

When you pray in this section of the model prayer, make sure your "Whole Armor of God" is in use. Pray holding nothing back. Confess everything. Petition God's rescue. Petition God's protection. Be confident in the fact that God answers prayer and that there is no problem, circumstance or situation too great or too small for Him to solve. He is waiting and willing to hear from you. He will provide a means of escape from the temptations that so easily beset you as soon as you trust and obey Him through His Son, our Lord Jesus Christ.

Matthew 6:13b
<u>For Thine Is The Kingdom, And The Power, And The Glory, Forever, Amen.</u>
Prayers of Praise and Thanksgiving

As the model prayer starts with praise and reverence to God, so does it end with praise, thanksgiving and reverence to God in this seventh and final segment of The Lord's Prayer.

"Thou art worthy, O Lord, to receive glory and honour and power: for Thou hast created all things, and for Thy pleasure they are and were created."
Revelation 4:11

God is worthy to be praised because His name is hallowed. He is righteousness, peace, joy in the Holy Spirit and power. His will is done in earth as it is in heaven. He gives us our daily bread. He sustains us. He forgives us as we forgive others. He leads us away from temptations. He frees us from wickedness. He is the Power. He is the Glory. He is the Creator of all things for His own pleasure. God is Alpha and Omega. God is the Great I AM. He is forever and ever. Praise, thank and show reverence to Him.

Jesus, in this model prayer, instructs you to echo the attributes of God that identify His kingdom. As stated before, these attributes can be found in the following two verses:

"For the kingdom of God are not meat and drink; but righteousness, and peace, and joy
in the Holy Ghost".
Romans 14:17

"For the kingdom of God is not in word, but in power."
Corinthians 4:20

God is a supernatural being above all beings. God through His Son, The Lord Jesus is King of kings and Lord of lords in the power of the Holy Ghost.

"For he is Lord of lords, and King of kings:"
Revelation 17:14b

When you pray in His presence at His Throne of Grace, as a way of life, be contrite and determined to accept His forgiveness. Maintain a heartfelt desire not to make the same errors over and over again. Be willing to seek forgiveness as well as to forgive others for their trespasses.

The only begotten Son of God, our Lord and Savior, Jesus Christ, paid the sin debt for us so that we may be made righteous in God's kingdom. Without the **Innocent Blood** that

Jesus shed, there is no hope for us to be a part of God's kingdom.

"And almost all things are by the law purged with blood; and without shedding of blood is no remission. . . .So Christ was once offered to bear the sins of many; and unto them that look for him shall he appear the second time without sin unto salvation."
Hebrews 9:22, 28

"For He hath made Him to be sin for us, who knew no sin; that we might be made the righteousness of God in Him."
2nd Corinthians 5:21

Not only is God righteous, peace, joy in the Holy Ghost, and power, He is Glory. God is Supreme Excellence. Therefore, He requires our best. His will is that we glorify Him in all we do. Exhort, honor and praise Him. The angels and heavenly host give glory to God.

"And suddenly there was with the angel a multitude of the heavenly host praising God,
and saying, Glory to God in the highest, and on earth peace, good will toward men."
Luke 2:13-14

If angels and heavenly host give glory to God, why not man on earth?

Having said all the above, if we could put our Lord's model prayer in a nutshell, it may include the following:

I.   Acknowledge God with reverence and Respect
(Our Father)

II.   Request God to reign in everyday living
(Thy kingdom come)

III.   Submit to His will in both heaven and earth **(Thy will be done)**

IV.   Make petitions, and intercessions known to Him for needed and desired provisions within His will
(Give us our daily bread)

V.   Confess sins, forgive others and ask for forgiveness from others
(Forgive us as we forgive others)

VI.   Petition needs of protection and rescue from immorality and all things outside God's will
(Lead us not into temptation but deliver us from evil)

VII.   Acknowledge the majesty of God and accept Him as the one and only power source for daily living
(For Our Father God is the Kingdom and the power and the glory for ever)

Our prayers at the very least should always include: praise for the righteousness of God, thanksgiving for the peace of God, submission to the power of God and His will in our daily life, petition and intercession for the blessings of God and joy in the Holy Ghost all to the glory of God.

At the beginning and at the conclusion of our prayers, honor, revere and magnify our Father, which is in heaven. He is the kingdom, the power and the glory forever, Amen.

A Prayer of Adoration, Praise and Thanksgiving

My Father God in Heaven, I lift my voice to You. You are the God of all gods. You are Alpha and Omega. You are my great protector for today and my hope for tomorrow. You are righteous and true. I can depend on You. Thank You, Lord for all You have done for me. All praises, honor and glory are Yours. I love you Lord and I lift my voice to You. Bless Your Holy Name. My Lord and my Father, I thank You for all Your blessings, grace and mercy toward me. But most of all I thank You for Your darling Son, The Lord Jesus, The Christ. Thank you for redemption through His precious blood. Glory to Your Name, in the Name of Jesus.

Amen

Chapter 8
Good Prayer Habits

*"Give ear to my words, O Lord, consider my
meditation. Hearken unto the voice of my cry,
my King, and my God: for unto Thee will I pray.
My voice shalt Thou hear in the morning O
Lord; in the morning will I direct my prayer unto
Thee, and will look up."*
Psalm 5:1-3

Good prayer habits are fertile ground for
spiritual growth and Christian maturity. Good
prayer habits evolve from regular communication with God. Good prayer habits are not
mystical or mysterious. Their origin is not
cryptic. They do not demand miraculous or
supernatural behaviors. Good prayer habits
develop by experiencing God on a regular basis.
Good prayer habits breed prayer effectiveness.
Prayer effectiveness is steered by sincerity, faith,
a repentant heart, and the willingness to submit
to God's will.

Since prayer is included as a form of
worship, pray in spirit. Pray in truth. The Bible
says,

*"... the true worshippers shall worship the
Father in spirit and in truth: for the Father*

seeketh such to worship him. God is a Spirit: and they that worship Him must worship Him in spirit and in truth."
John 4:23b-24

Good prayer habits involve positive motives and attitudes. Obedient submissiveness to the only true and Living God demonstrates positive motives and attitudes.

A solid prerequisite for the development of true worship and good prayer habits is found in the sixth chapter of Ephesians.

"Put on the whole armour of God that ye may be able to stand against the wiles of the devil. For we wrestle not against flesh and blood, but against principalities, against powers, against the rulers of the darkness of this world, against spiritual wickedness in high places. Wherefore take unto you the whole armour of God that ye may be able to withstand in the evil day, and having done all, to stand. Stand therefore, having your loins girt about with truth, and having on the breastplate of righteousness; And your feet shod with the preparation of the gospel of peace; Above all, taking the shield of faith, wherewith ye shall be able to quench all the fiery darts of the wicked. And take the helmet of salvation, and the sword of the Spirit, which is

the word of God: <u>*Praying always with all prayer and supplication in the Spirit,*</u> *"*
Ephesians 6:11-18a

The Whole Armour of God is Jesus, the Messiah, the Christ, and the indwelling of the Holy Spirit within each believer. If allowed, He will girt your loins with truth as you wrestle against principalities, powers and rulers of the darkness of this world. He will be your breastplate of righteousness when you come against spiritual wickedness in high places. He will prepare you for the gospel of peace so that you may be able to withstand the evils of each day. He will shield your body with faith so you may quench all the fiery darts of the wicked one. He will cover your head with salvation and give you the sword of the Spirit, which is the word of God. He will always encourage you to pray in the Spirit with sincerity for yourself and others.

Jesus is the believer's protector against the rulers of darkness of this world and against spiritual wickedness in high places. When you are wrapped in the Whole Armour of God, you can stand fast against everything outside God's will. Put on the Whole Armour of God; put on Jesus.

"But God commendeth his love toward us, in that, while we were yet sinners, Christ died for us. Much more then, being now justified by His

blood, we shall be saved from wrath through Him."
Romans 5:8-9

When you wrap yourself in Jesus, as the Whole Armour of God, you will be able to stand against the wiles of the devil. Therefore, the standard for a good prayer life is as follows:

Truth

A pray(er) at the Throne of Grace in the presence of God must have integrity.   It is essential for the pray(er) to be honest and genuine in his communication with God.

"Behold, thou (God) desirest truth in the inward parts (the heart of man):"
Psalm 51:6a

Keep your loins girded with truth. God hates lies and dishonesty.

"...and love no false oath: for all these are things that I hate, saith the Lord."
Zechariah 8:17b

Righteousness:

Righteousness is strict observance to God's laws, statutes and ordinances. It is a blame-lessness through faith from the penalty of sin. It is God's justification through His Son, Jesus Christ, for the penalty of sin. A pray(er) at the Throne of Grace, necessitates righteousness in

God's sight, through Jesus, before there can be any positive communication between God and the pray(er).

"For the righteous Lord loveth righteousness; his countenance doth behold the upright."
Psalm 11:7

"Thou (God) lovest righteousness, and hatest wickedness:
Psalm 45:7

The breastplate of righteousness *(that only comes through your belief in the life, death, burial, resurrection, and ascension of Jesus with the promise of His return)* keeps your heart *(your very essence)* from the wiles of the evil one. The righteousness of God in you through Jesus, is essential when praying in the will of God at His Throne of Grace.

The gospel of Peace:

A pray(er) at the Throne of God's Grace, demonstrates full confidence in Jesus. That is, a pray(er) rests in the knowledge that Jesus has given His peace. Because of the peace given by Jesus, the pray(er) does not worry. He is not afraid of the wickedness of the world as he proclaims the Gospel. He knows that God is our protector and our provider. He knows that God will answer prayers according to His will for each believer.

"Peace I leave with you, my peace I give unto you: not as the world giveth, give I unto you.
Let not your heart be troubled, neither let it be afraid."
John 14:27

Faith:

A pray(er) in the presence of God has complete trust in God, knowing beyond a shadow of doubt that God's response to prayer is the best for any given situation. He knows that God has given all believers a portion of faith and that God is faithful and just to forgive sins and to cleanse from all unrighteousness. God will hear the pray(er) when he prays because of the pray(ers) belief in Jesus. The faith the pray(er) has in God through the love of Jesus will shield him from the fiery darts of the evil one.

"Above all, taking the shield of faith,"
Ephesians 6:16a

Salvation:

A pray(er) in the presence of God at His Throne of Grace knows and understands that he has been delivered from deserved punishment due to sins. He knows that he has been mercifully showered with undeserved favor from God by the crucifixion of Jesus and is now saved not by self-works but by God's grace.

Jesus, our Salvation, is the one and only mediator between God and man. Salvation affirms obedience, in addition to adherence to the Holy Scriptures as the way of life for all believers. Salvation is the helmet of all believers. The helmet of salvation protects the mind and allows thoughts to be rooted in Jesus. Accept the protection salvation offers. Believe that Jesus is the only begotten son of the Living God. When you pray, He will be the mediator between you and God.

Sword of the Spirit, which is The Word of God:

A pray(er) who approaches God at His Throne of Grace prays the word of God in his prayers. The Bible says,

"For the word of God is quick, and powerful, and sharper than any two-edged sword, piercing even to the dividing asunder of soul and spirit, and of the joints and marrow, and is a discerner of the thoughts and intents of the heart."
Hebrews 4:12

The word of God, which is the Sword of the Spirit never returns to God void. It is a discerner of the thoughts and intents of the heart. When you drape yourself in the Whole Armour of God, with the Sword of the Spirit at your side, you will speak the known words of God found in the

Bible in spirit and in truth. You will live in obedience to God's commandments, statutes and precepts.

Not only does this approach to prayer keep you within the will of God, it also makes your prayer requests clearer. God will respond to His words. Bible study and meditation are imperative at this level of prayer as you hold the *Sword of the Spirit* in your daily life. The Sword of the Spirit, the word of God is a powerful tool against the wiles of the devil.

Praying all prayer with supplication in the Spirit:

A pray(er) in the presence of God at His Throne of Grace, prays all seven components of The Lord's Prayer with supplication. These components are prayers of adoration (worship), praise and thanksgiving, submission, petition, confession, and intercession. Supplication as stated earlier in this book is clearly described in Romans 12:1. The total body, mind and soul must be humbly presented as a living sacrifice to God, which is your reasonable service; as prayer is to be rendered in the Spirit.

Believers in God through Jesus Christ dress themselves daily with The Whole Armour of God. With this armour, they are protected against Satan who is always shooting his fiery darts of damnation at each believer. Without this protection, the devil is sure to hit his mark and strike a deadly blow eventually. Do not find yourself anywhere without Jesus, The Whole Armour of God. He is your protection *"against the wiles of the devil, against principalities, against powers, against the rulers of the darkness of this world, and against spiritual wickedness in high places."*

Keep your communication with God open at all times. God sets no specific times of the day for pray(ers) to talk with Him. Neither are there any specific places to pray. God is available to hear and communicate with you 24 hours of every day and 7 days of every week, all the time, at any place. Take advantage of this privilege.

It is a good thing to keep God through Jesus Christ on your mind in every situation. David in Psalm 55:17 said,

"Evening, and morning, and at noon, will I pray, and cry aloud: and He shall hear my voice."

Traditionally many Christians pray upon arising each day. They thank and praise God for the morning's awakening and the sleep of the night before.

"It is a good thing to give thanks unto the Lord, and to sing praises unto thy name, O most High:

*To shew forth thy lovingkindness in the morning,
and thy faithfulness every night,"*
Psalm 92:1-2

During this time, prayers for God's blessings upon loved ones and for self are prayed. Intercessions for the sick, afflicted, shut-in, incarcerated, international governments, national, and local leaders are made. Direction of the Holy Spirit is petitioned for the entire day.

"Cause me to hear thy lovingkindness in the morning; for in thee do I trust: cause me to know the way wherein I should walk; for I lift up my soul unto thee."
Psalm 143:8

There are at least two other traditional times for daily prayer. They are before eating and just before retiring for sleep at the end of your day. At each meal, Christians praise God for the food before them. They pray for His blessings upon the food provided for physical nourishment. They may also pray for the preparer of the food and the hands that serve it. At bedtime, they thank God for the day and prayer for His protection during their time of slumber.

"Thus will I bless Thee while I live: I will lift up my hands in Thy name. My soul shall be satisfied as with marrow and fatness; and my mouth shall praise Thee with joyful lips: When I remember

*Thee upon my bed, and meditate on Thee in the
night watches."*
Psalm 63:4-6

In addition to these traditions, Christians
who have a strong relationship with God tend to
have a regular time of personal devotion, which
includes Bible study, meditation and prayer at
least once a day. The more you study God's
Word and the more you pray, the easier it will be
for you to develop a positive relationship with
God and continue to grow and mature in His way
of life for you.

If at first good prayer habits along with
Bible study and devotion seem difficult for you,
here is a suggestion. Do not allow your mind to
wander. Stay focused. If you continue to find it
hard to concentrate, perhaps this simple prayer
will help with intentional deliberation on God's
word. Just repeat the following prayer or one
similar until strength to focus on God's word
occurs.

*Father, in the name of Jesus, speak to me
through Your word. Let me delight in Your law,
and let me understand Your word for me this day,
Amen.*

In this brief prayer, you are repeating His word
found in Psalm 1:2.

Meditation during devotion is simply

focusing on God through faith in Jesus Christ. It is tuning out all surroundings and concentrating on God for hearing and understanding His Word. Meditation is exercising total awareness of nothing but thoughts of God through His Word. If at first you find it hard to meditate, try this. Say in all sincerity the brief prayer below until you can concentrate solely on the Word of God.

Father, in the name of Jesus, I come to Your Throne of Grace. Let Your words abide in me. Let me understand and meditate on Your words Amen.

Do not recite these words with your lips only, but speak them from your heart. Say this prayer until you find yourself transformed from your physical surroundings to the Throne of Grace in the presence of the Lord. At this time, you may also repeat His word to Him. Here is at least one scripture verse you may use.

"Let the words of my mouth, and the meditation of my heart, be acceptable in thy sight, O Lord, my strength, and my redeemer."
Psalm 19:14

Conduct devotion at a definite place where meditation, study, and prayer may not be interrupted. Encourage family to share in this time of devotion, prayer and Bible study with you. If this is impossible at home, perhaps it may be done in a quiet room at a place of worship or the neighborhood public library or even a quiet booth at a favorite restaurant. Be reminded that it's not the physical place of which you devote time with God in study and prayer, it is your spiritual whereabouts that count.

It should also be determined at what time of each day your personal devotions with God will take place. The amount of time in devotion may be flexible. It is solely based on the time you want to spend on forming a relationship with God through prayer. If it is found that no time for devotion is available, it is likely that too much time for routine tasks and other stuff of a lesser priority are interfering with the development of your positive relationship with God. Pray to God, your Father, through Jesus Christ, that priorities are set according to His will for a strong relationship with Him. Use the Armour of God recorded in Ephesians 6:11-18 and highlighted in this chapter to overcome the wiles of the evil one regarding your personal time with God.

As time with God continues, begin to set goals and objectives for these cherished moments with Him. Maturity in Christianity is a step-by-step process that demands Communication with God. Tell Him all about your letdowns and triumphs. Tell Him about your needs and desires, your hopes and dreams. Ask for wisdom and knowledge in Him. Request that He direct your day. Pour your heart out to Him. Christian growth is developed through successes and failures, trials and errors. Do not be afraid to share your blunders with Him. Share your total being with God. Seek guidance on how to overcome challenges, and how to recover from attacks of the evil one. If you are specific in your prayers, God will be specific in His reply to you. Study the Bible, meditate, pray and listen for His small still voice in your heart. Act on His will for you.

*"I listen to God as I read His Word. I speak to
Him through meditation and prayer.
I say exactly what is in my heart to say.
He answers me through His word
in His own way."*
Curtis Evans

Keep channels open for regular and instant communication with God all the time by means of devotion, Bible study and prayer. It has often been said,

*"Never study the Bible without prayer
and never pray without reading God's word."
and
"Devotion without prayer
is like a body without a soul."*

Bible study, prayer, meditation, and devotion are vital for the true believer in Christ.

Briefly, here is a systematic simple way to develop good prayer habits.

1) Institute daily quiet times for coming before God's Throne of Grace, in His presence for devotion and prayer.

2) Pray for understanding of God's word and His will in your life.

3) Read the Bible and meditate on His words regularly.

4) Praise God in prayer for His daily goodness, grace and mercy showered upon you and those for which you intercede.

5) Pray for specific concerns and His presence in your life. Do not overlook prayer about successes as well as failures, joys as well as sorrows.

6) Pray for family, friends, associates, neighbors, community, local, national and, international government officials.

7) Praise God through Jesus Christ for His goodness and mercy, and for His righteousness, peace, joy, power and strength in your life.

Continue your day with God in your heart, confident that He abides with you and that He truly answers prayer.

Pray the prayer that Christians do, and may the
Whole Armour of God
through Jesus Christ, rest upon you.
Curtis Evans

Chapter 9
Benefits of Prayer

"Blessed be the Lord,
who daily loadeth us with benefits,
even the God of our salvation. Selah."
Psalm 68:19

In the world today, benefits are often thought of in terms of monetary concerns. In actuality, benefits are advantages that may exceed financial gain. Fringe benefits *assistance for the livelihood of employees but not actualized in net wages or salary),* include paid health insurance, paid vacation days, holiday pay and other pecuniary contributions provided for time spent and service rendered at a specific place of employment.

Social Security and pension are monetary benefits. Trusts, endowments, and grants may be monetary benefits. Disability, unemployment compensation, various insurance, legal payouts and charitable benevolence also may come in the form of monetary benefits. Procurement of monetary benefits in our current society has become a multi-billion dollar industry. More frequently than not, our world equates benefits with money. Seldom are non-monetary advantages held at the same level of esteem as advantages that have money attached to them.

In this world of graft and greed, moral advantages such as compassion, kindness, and loving consideration for fellowmen seem to be of no accepted value. One may think that these human traits are useless. In many circles, they are scorned. Nevertheless, these advantages are encouraged by God. They are often referred to as theological virtues. Regardless of worldly views, characteristics identified as faith, hope and charity are necessities for all Christians. Such virtues are vividly expressed in what is called the *"Love Chapter"* of the New Testament. They are found in the book of 1st Corinthians chapter 13 verse 13.

Faith: steadfast belief in God through Jesus Christ

Hope: expectation of all the blessings of God, especially the second coming of Jesus

Charity: compassion, kindness, empathy and unconditional love for all men

Godly benefits of prayer are grounded in steadfast belief in God through Jesus. They are rooted in the expectation that all blessings are of God. God's blessings are like beautiful flowers that bloom with compassion, kindness, empathy and love for all humanity. These three benefits of God are moral qualities that far exceed any advantage the world may give. Neither can man quantify them in terms of currency. Yet when forming a relationship with God through prayer, they are priceless. They are observably strong indicators of Christian maturity. Faith, hope and charity *(generosity in helping and giving from a heart of kindness, compassion and confidence in God)* are prominent parts of the character of all who come in the presence of God at His Throne of Grace for prayer. These moral behaviors must not be ignored in a Christian's daily life.

Prayers backed by these traits are true markers for the possibility of answered prayer. They bring with them praise and thanksgiving worthy of God's benefits. Read The Holy Bible regularly and see God's benefits revealed. Psalm 103, a song of thanksgiving written by King David, emphasizes advantages given to man because of God's grace and mercy. Advantages found in this psalm are both physical and spiritual. In this division of the book of Psalms, Psalm 103, is divided into four sections. Each section provides an insight of the goodness of God toward us:

1) the introduction and prerequisite for bene-
    fits and blessings from God, our Father,
    verses 1 - 2

2) benefits from God, our Father, due to His grace and mercy,
   verses 3 9

3) benefits from God, our Father, as from an earthly father to his children,
   verses 10 - 18

4) benefits of God, our Father, in heaven for a time to come.
   verses 19 - 22

Introduction and prerequisite

"Bless the Lord, O my soul: and all that is within me, bless His holy name. Bless the Lord, O my soul, and forget not all His benefits:"
Psalm 103:1-2

To *bless the Lord* means to pronounce happiness in God because God is Consecrated and Holy. His name is Hallowed. When saying, 'bless the Lord,' it brings jubilance to the soul. Psalm 103, verses one and two starts out with these words that motivate an atmosphere of inner joy. Bless the Lord with all that is within, from the breadth, and length, and depth, and height of hearts and souls! Thank, praise and glorify the Lord. Revere Him. Honor Him because He is God and beside Him, there is no other. His benefits are abundant. They are always. They are for now and they are forever. Thank and praise Him at all times for all His goodness.

Never forget the benefits of a positive relationship with Him. Bless the Lord. He introduces true peace and joy, righteousness and power in all situations.

Benefits of God due to His Grace and Mercy

"Who forgiveth all thine iniquities; who healeth all thy diseases; Who redeemeth thy life from destruction; who crowneth thee with loving-kindness and tender mercies; Who satisfieth thy mouth with good things; so that thy youth is renewed like the eagle's. The Lord executeth righteousness and judgment for all that are oppressed. He made known His ways unto Moses, His acts unto the children of Israel. The Lord is merciful and gracious, slow to anger, and plenteous in mercy. He will not always chide: neither will He keep His anger forever."
Psalm 103:3-9

There are at least eleven benefits found in the preceding verses. Each one is offered to all believers in God through His Son, Jesus Christ.

1) **who forgiveth all thine iniquities:**
God forgives sin. The God we pray to is the ***Absolute Pardoner*** of sin.

"...thou art a God ready to pardon, gracious and merciful, slow to anger, and of great kindness,..."
Nehemiah 9:17d

"Seek ye the Lord while He may be found, call ye upon Him while He is near: Let the wicked forsake his way, and the unrighteous man his thoughts: and let him return unto the Lord, and He will have mercy upon him; and to our God, for He will abundantly pardon."
Isaiah 55:6-7

You may be reminded of a request for this benefit in the Model Prayer often called The Lord's Prayer. **"Forgive us our debts."** God can forgive. He pardons sin. Just ask Him. What a benefit!

2) **who healeth all thy diseases:**
God heals all our diseases. The God we pray to is The *Devine Healer, Jehovah-Rapha,* the only One who can heal diseases of the physical body and the sin-sickened soul. To every believer, God offers the benefit of healing. He can heal the sick and He can save the sinner.

"And the prayer of faith shall save the sick, and the Lord shall raise him up; and if he have committed sins, they shall be forgiven him."
James 5:15

Pray believing that God hears and answers prayer.

3) **who redeemeth thy life from destruction:**
God redeems us from destruction. The God we pray to is The *Redeemer from Destruction:*

*"He sent his word, and healed them, and deliver-
ed them from their destructions. Oh that men
would praise the Lord for His goodness, and for
His wonderful works to the children of men!"*
Psalm 107:20-21

*"It is of the Lord's mercies that we are not
consumed because His compassions fail not.*
Lamentations 3:22

*"In whom we have redemption through His
blood, the forgiveness of sins, according to the
riches of His grace;"*
Ephesians 1:7

Pray the prayer that Jesus taught in faith and
action. ***"Lead us not into temptation, but deliver
us from evil."***

4)   <u>**who crowneth thee with loving kindness
and tender mercies:**</u>
God fills us up with His loving kindness and His
tender mercies. The God we pray to is
***The Bottomless Well of Loving Kindness and
Tender Mercies.***

*"For His merciful kindness is great toward us:
and the truth of the Lord endureth forever. Praise
ye the Lord."*
Psalms 117:2

Pray for the benefit of loving kindness and
tender mercies in your life. God gives them

freely to all who ask in faith.

5) **who satisfieth thy mouth with good things; so that thy youth is renewed like the eagle's.**

God satisfies physical bodies with good things and renews youth. The God we pray to is *The Faithful Provider.* He is called *Jehovah Jireh and Jehovah-Rohi*. He nourishes and sustains daily. King David said,

"It is God that girdeth me with strength, and maketh my way perfect."
Psalm 18:32

King Solomon said,

"...give me neither poverty nor riches; feed me with food convenient for me:"
Proverbs 30:8b

Jesus taught His disciples to say,

"Give us this day our daily bread."
Matthew 6:11

6) **The Lord executeth righteousness and judgment for all that are oppressed. He made known His ways unto Moses, His acts unto the children of Israel.**

God righteously vindicates the oppressed. The God we pray to is **The Righteous Judge.**

"For He shall deliver the needy when he crieth; the poor also, and him that hath no helper. He shall spare the poor and needy, and shall save the souls of the needy."
Psalm 72:12-13

God The Righteous Judge "**delivers us from evil**." Trust Him. Develop a prayer life with Him.

7) <u>merciful and gracious</u>

God is compassionate and kind. The God we pray to is **The God of Great Empathy.** He knows and understands our feelings. He is humane in His response when we pray to Him.

"But thou, O Lord, art a God full of compassion, and gracious, longsuffering, and plenteous in mercy and truth."
Psalm 86:15

God knows the innermost chambers of the heart. He cares. He understands. He has compassion. In prayer, pour out your innermost concerns to Him. He will not fail you.

8) <u>slow to anger</u>

God is slow to anger. The God we pray to is **The God of Patience.** He is tolerant and deliberate in His behavior. A scripture in this same passage states that, '**He will not always chide.**' God, our Father, is bountiful in mercy.

He does not always reprimand. He is righteous and He is just. His actions are determined by His will and way for us.

"The Lord is gracious, and full of compassion; slow to anger, and of great mercy. The Lord is good to all: and His tender mercies are over all His works."
Psalm 145:8-9

When you feel your sin is too great to ask for forgiveness, know that God does not get angry easily. He does correct. He also forgives. Do not be afraid to tell Him all. He is your Heavenly Father; He knows how to handle all situations without anger.

9) **and plenteous in mercy:**

The scriptures declare His mercy over and over. He abundantly pardons those who deserve punishment. The God we pray to is **The Compassionate King** for all who accept Him.

"But he, being full of compassion, forgave their iniquity, and destroyed them not: yea, many a time turned he his anger away, and did not stir up all his wrath."
Psalm 78:38

Call upon Him in prayer; He is plenteous in mercy and compassion.

10) **He will not always chide:**

The God we pray to is **The Calm Corrector.** He

is compassionate and merciful when scolding is necessary. His correction is not heated with anger. He corrected Adam and Eve in the cool of the day. God corrected Jonah by the shadow of a gourd.

"My son, despise not the chastening of the Lord; neither be weary of His correction: For whom the Lord loveth He correcteth; even as a father the son in whom He delighteth."
Proverbs 3:11-12

Pray for God's will in your life, realizing you cannot mature in Him without correction from time to time. **'Let Thy will be done in earth as it is in heaven' and 'But deliver us from evil'** come to mind in this instance. What a benefit in knowing that God's will can be done in our lives. In addition, He is able to deliver us from the evils of this world.

11) **neither will He keep His anger forever.** Although, The God we pray to is **The God of Patience,** He will not always withdraw His anger from us. Our God is also The **Detester of Disobedience.** He does not always quench His wrath.

"Let no man deceive you with vain words: for because of these things cometh the wrath of God upon the children of disobedience."
Ephesians 5:6

"For the wrath of God is revealed from heaven against all ungodliness and unrighteousness of men, who hold the truth in unrighteousness;" Romans 1:18

"He that believeth on the Son hath everlasting life: and he that believeth not the Son shall not see life; but the wrath of God abideth on him." John 3:36

God does not always keep His anger. God does correct. And whomever He corrects He loves. *Read Proverbs 3:11-12 on preceding page.*

What an encouragement to know that the God of the entire universe will take the time to lead, guide and correct us according to His gracious mercies. How reassuring it is to know that the benefits of God, our Father, through Christ Jesus are always available. Believe and obey His will. Accept His promises. Live in His way. Pray to Him and be blessed.

What you have read is just the beginning. Praying in the presence of God as a way of life most definitely offers benefits. Here are some more benefits from the same psalm.

Benefits from God as from an earthly father to his children

"He hath not dealt with us after our sins; nor rewarded us according to our iniquities. For as the heaven is high above the earth, so great is

His mercy toward them that fear him. As far as the east is from the west, so far hath He removed our transgressions from us. Like as a father pitieth his children, so the Lord pitieth them that fear Him. For He knoweth our frame; He remembereth that we are dust. As for man, his days are as grass: as a flower of the field, so he flourisheth. For the wind passeth over it, and it is gone; and the place thereof shall know it no more. But the mercy of the Lord is from everlasting to everlasting upon them that fear Him, and His righteousness unto children's children; To such as keep His covenant, and to those that remember His commandments to do them."
Psalm 103:10-18

In the verses just mentioned, God's benefits continue as an earthly father to his children, compassionate and true. They are as follows.

a) God forgives and pardons sin.
b) God has empathy for all who fear *(revere)* Him.
c) God of the entire universe knows us all one by one.
d) God knows our qualities and imperfections.
e) God's mercy is everlasting.
f) God is forever righteous toward each of us.
g) God encourages us to keep His covenant and to do His commandments.

The God we pray to is Our Father in Heaven. He is **The Perfect Parent.** He is kind, gracious and merciful. He offers favor upon us for things we have not merited. This action is called God's grace. He grants pardons for punishment we justly deserve. This action is called mercy. God is abundant with kindness and plentiful with compassion. God is gracious and merciful. By the blood of Jesus, He can take away our individual sins. Everyone who believes in God, our Father, and His Son has the benefit of an everlasting life through the power of His grace and mercy.

"And after all that is come upon us for our evil deeds, and for our great trespass, seeing that thou our God hast punished us less than our iniquities deserve, and hast given us such deliverance as this;"
Ezra 9:13

Our Father, God is ever faithful, gracious and merciful. He lavishes us with grace and mercy every day.

"They (God's mercies and compassions) are new every morning: great is thy faithfulness."
Lamentations 3:23

"I thank my God always on your behalf, for the grace of God which is given you by Jesus Christ; That in everything ye are enriched by him, in all

utterance, and in all knowledge;"
1ˢᵗ Corinthians 1:4-5

"Let us therefore come boldly unto the throne of grace that we may obtain mercy, and find grace to help in time of need."
Hebrews 4:16

God, our Heavenly Father, knows the character and frailties of each one of his children and has compassion upon each one accordingly. His compassion is eternal. He knows each child's innermost beings. He cares for each one individually. He knows each one's make up and He remembers where each child came from. He even knows the number of hairs on each one's head.

"But the very hairs of your head are all num-bered."
Matthew 10:30

He knows when you came in this world. He knows when your time on this earth will end. Associates, neighbors, friends and many family members will lose memory of you when you are gone. However, God is your all loving Holy Perfect Parent, He never forgets. He made you and He will not forget you. His kindness and mercy is from everlasting to everlasting. To receive His benefits, do His commandments and hold fast to His promises.

In the Bible, there are many promises that The Holy Trinity makes to man. Three examples of God's promises are detailed as follows. Each example is designed to assist you to continue in the development of Christian maturity. They are all conditional. That is the promise will only materialize after certain specifics are done by you. If you do something, one of the characteristics of the Triune God will do something in regards to what you have done.

(IF) "If ye love me (Jesus), (THEN) keep my commandments. And I will pray the Father, and He (God) shall give you another Comforter, that He (The Holy Spirit) may abide with you forever;"
John 14:15-16

The conditions are to love Jesus and keep His commandments. If these conditions are met, then the promise in this verse is threefold:

1) Jesus, the Son of God, will intercede for you to God
2) God the Father will give you another Comforter
3) The Holy Spirit *(The Comforter)* will live with you forever.

(THEN) "And whatsoever we ask, we receive of Him (God),because (IF) we keep His (Jesus) commandments, and do those things that are

pleasing in His (God) sight."
1ˢᵗ John 3:22

In this verse the conditions are:

1) to keep the commandments of Jesus (Read 1ˢᵗ John 3:23, 24) and
2) to do what is pleasing in the sight of Almighty God.

If these two conditions are satisfied then God, through Jesus Christ, will give you whatsoever things are pleasing in His sight.

(IF) "But he that shall endure unto the end, (THEN) the same shall be saved."
Matthew 24:13

The last example reminds you that the promises of God are life-long and has everlasting benefits. *If* you endure to the end, **then** you shall be saved. This is ultimate benefit given to man by God through Jesus.

The suggested readings portion of this book identifies a few books to read that may be of value to you concerning praying the promises of God. They will focus on passages of scripture that show how God leads, guides and directs His children to righteousness, peace, joy in the Spirit and power from on high. God, through His Son, Jesus is truly the Perfect Parent. Keep open your line of communication with Him. He answers prayer.

<u>Benefits of God our Father in heaven for a time to come</u>

"The Lord hath prepared His throne in the heavens; and His kingdom ruleth over all. Bless the Lord, ye His angels, that excels in strength, that does his commandments, hearkening unto the voice of His word. Bless ye the Lord, all ye His hosts; ye ministers of His that do his pleasure. Bless the Lord, all His works in all places of His dominion: bless the Lord, O my soul."
Psalm 103:19-22

God's benefits continue into His eternity for each believer. He has prepared His throne in His kingdom to rule over each of us. In these final verses of the 103rd Psalm, God identifies some of His future benefits for us. His angels are happy to carry out His orders, will excel in His strength, do His commandments, and listen closely to His words. In God's kingdom to come, His hosts and His ministers do His pleasure. In God's kingdom to come all His dominion, everything and everywhere, will bless *(praise and glorify)* Him.

My soul will bless the Lord, of Heaven in His kingdom of righteousness, peace, joy in the Holy Ghost and power.
What a benefit to praise God forever and ever!

Just as the Model or Lord's Prayer instructs, this psalm also starts out with reverence and praises to God for His benefits on earth and it ends with praises of His power and majesty in His kingdom to come. May we forever glorify His Name. **"For He is the Kingdom, and the Power and the Glory forever and ever."**

The blessings of God are benefits beyond compare. Why not accept them as you communicate with Him! If scripture references above are not enough for you to believe in the benefits of prayer, here are a few more examples of God's benefits as stated in His Word, The Holy Bible. These benefits confirm God's loving-kindness and compassion for you now and in the world to come.

"Ask, and it shall be given you; seek, and ye shall find; knock, and it shall be opened unto you: For every one that asketh receiveth; and he that seeketh findeth; and to him that knocketh it shall be opened."
Matthew 7:7-8

"If any of you lack wisdom, let him ask of God, that giveth to all men liberally, and upbraideth not; and it shall be given him."
James 1:5

"And all things, whatsoever ye shall ask in prayer, believing, ye shall receive."
Matthew 21:22

"And this is the confidence that we have in Him that, if we ask any thing according to His will, He heareth us; And if we know that He hear us, whatsoever we ask, we know that we have the petitions that we desired of Him."
1ˢᵗ John 5:14-15

"Then shall ye call upon me, and ye shall go and pray unto me, and I will hearken unto you."
Jeremiah 29:12

"Now therefore hearken unto Me, O ye children: for blessed are they that keep my ways."
Proverbs 8:32

"But as it is written, Eye hath not seen, nor ear heard, neither has entered into the heart of man, the things which God hath prepared for them that love him."
1ˢᵗ Corinthians 2:9

Chapter 10
Frequently Asked Questions About Prayer

1) When we pray to whom do we pray?
Karah of Huntsville, Alabama

Follow the Model or Lord's Prayer.

*"After this manner therefore pray ye: **Our Father** which art in heaven, Hallowed be thy name."*
Matthew 6:9

Pray, "Our Father," while at the same time being knowledgeable of the fact that we serve a Triune God: God the Father, God the Son and God the Holy Ghost. They are all in One. They are all attentive to our prayers. God, The Holy Ghost guides us in our prayers. God, the Son (our Lord and Savior, Jesus Christ) intercedes for us during prayer and God the Father answers our prayers.

Many pray(ers) start their prayers in this way, **"Our Father",** and they conclude their prayers with these words, **"In the Name of Jesus, Amen**."

2) <u>Does God hear a sinner's prayer?</u>
Kayla of Huntsville, Alabama

If God does not hear a sinner's prayer, not one of us has a hope for eternal life with Him.

"For all have sinned, and come short of the glory of God;"
Romans 3:23

At a time before becoming a Christian, every current Christian had to pray a sinner's prayer. This prayer is a prayer and supplication of confession with a plea for forgiveness. It is a prayer of submission, and it is a prayer of adoration and thanks.

Since the fall of Adam, all of us have been born into a sinful state. From that time forward, God has desired to transform us, His creation from sinner to saint. The beginning of this transformation starts with the sinners' prayer. Let the sinner call upon God. God wants to hear from him. Yes, God does hear a sinner's prayer.

"Two men went up into the temple to pray; the one a Pharisee (those who insisted on strict observance of Jewish ritual laws), and the other a publican (tax collector usually despised by fellow Jews) The Pharisee stood and prayed. . . And the publican, standing afar off, would not lift up so much as his eyes unto heaven, but smote upon his breast, saying, God be merciful to me a

sinner. . . I tell you, this man went down to his house justified rather than the other:" Read Luke 18:10-17 in its entirety.

3) Should I pray for revenge?
Katherine of Huntsville, Alabama

There are many instances in the Old Testament where people of God prayed for vengeance upon their enemies. In the Book of Psalms, we can see several prayers requesting punishment for enemies. However, most of the revenge prayers were primarily prompted during times of war. The following scripture is a statement about vengeance.

"To Me (God) belongeth vengeance and recompence;..."
Deuteronomy 32:35a

One of the primary goals in Christian life is to love and not hate or hold grudges. In the New Testament, we will find a recurring theme that challenges us to love and forgive one another. Jesus said:

"But I say unto you, Love your enemies, bless them that curse you, do good to them that hate you, and pray for them which despitefully use you, and persecute you;"
Matthew 5:44

Pray for a change in the life of the one who has done you wrong. Pray so that God through Jesus Christ may bring them to the realization that they too need to be saved. Pray that the errors of their ways be revealed to them and that they may have the courage to make adjustments according to the will of God. Keep this verse in your heart when thinking in terms of revenge.

"I exhort therefore, that, first of all, supplications, prayers, intercessions, and giving of thanks, be made for all men; For kings, and for all that are in authority; that we may lead a quiet and peaceable life in all godliness and honesty. For this is good and acceptable in the sight of God our Saviour;
1ˢᵗ Timothy 2:1-3;

Here are a couple of Bible verses concerning love over vengeance.

"Dearly beloved, avenge not yourselves, but rather give place unto wrath: for it is written, Vengeance is mine; I will repay, saith the Lord. Therefore, if thine enemy hunger, feed him; if he thirst, give him drink: for in so doing thou shalt heap coals of fire on his head. Be not overcome of evil, but overcome evil with good."
Romans 12:19-21

"For we know Him that hath said, Vengeance belongeth unto Me, I will recompense, saith the Lord. And again, The Lord shall judge his people."
Hebrews 10:30

Vengeance is the Lord's. We should not pray for vengeance. Instead, pray to God for relief of the situation and a changed heart for those who despitefully use and persecute you. God knows just what to do.

4) Is it all right to intercede for others without their knowledge?
Mary, St. Louis, Missouri

To pray in the presence of God at His Throne of Grace, is to pray under the guidance of our Triune God. The Holy Spirit may guide you to pray for others without their knowledge. Interceding in prayer by Christians for others is not an uncommon action. While on earth, Jesus interceded in prayer for us. Here are a couple of noted examples.

1)... *"Then said Jesus, Father, forgive them; for they know not what they do."*
Luke 23:34

In the preceding verse, Jesus interceded in prayer for those who crucified Him. Surely, they had no expectations of His prayer for them.

2)   *"Neither pray I for these alone, but for*
     them also which shall believe on me
     through their word;"
     John 17:20

In the afore stated verse, Jesus interceded in prayer not only for the disciples who walked and talked with Him on earth, but He also prayed for believers who were yet to come. That is, if you are a believer, Jesus prayed for you before you were born. Even now, in heaven, Jesus continues to intercede for you.

"For there is one God, and one mediator be-
tween God and men, The Man, Christ Jesus;
Who gave Himself a ransom for all, to be
testified in due time."
1ˢᵗ Timothy 2: 5-6

Most definitely, we are encouraged to intercede in prayer for others.

"Be kindly affectioned one to another with
brotherly love; in honour preferring one
another; Not slothful in business; fervent in
spirit; serving the Lord; Rejoicing in hope;
patient in tribulation; continuing instant in
prayer."
Romans 12:10-12

It is appropriate to intercede in prayer for others, even without their knowledge.

5)   **Should we pray for the dead and especially the unsaved dead?**
Gloria, Las Vegas Nevada

The Bible does not teach that Christians should intercede in prayer for the dead. The priority of God through His Son, Jesus Christ is focused on the unsaved living, not the dead. There is a passage in scripture where one dead person speaks with another dead person. Read what the scripture says:

"And there was a certain beggar named Lazarus, which was laid at his gate, full of sores, And desiring to be fed with the crumbs which fell from the rich man's table: more-over the dogs came and licked his sores. And it came to pass, that the beggar died, and was carried by the angels into Abraham's bosom: the rich man also died, and was buried; And in hell he lift up his eyes, being in torments, and seeth Abraham afar off, and Lazarus in his bosom. And he cried and said, Father Abraham, have mercy on me, and send Lazarus, that he may dip the tip of his finger in water, and cool my tongue; for I am tormented in this flame. But Abraham said, Son, remember that thou in thy lifetime receivedst thy good things, and likewise Lazarus evil things: but now he is comforted, and thou art tormented. And beside all this, between us and you there is a great gulf fixed: so that they which would pass

from hence to you cannot; neither can they pass to us, that would come from thence. Then he said, I pray thee therefore, father, that thou wouldest send him to my father's house: For I have five brethren; that he may testify unto them, lest they also come into this place of torment. Abraham saith unto him, They have Moses and the prophets; let them hear them. And he said, Nay, father Abraham: but if one went unto them from the dead, they will repent. And he said unto him, If they hear not Moses and the prophets, neither will they be persuaded, though one rose from the dead."
Luke 16:20-31

Following are two other scripture verses that may shed some light concerning the question of praying for the dead.

1) *"And another of His disciples said unto him, Lord, suffer me first to go and bury my father. But Jesus said unto him, Follow Me; and let the dead bury their dead."*
Matthew 8:21-22

2) *"And he said unto another, follow me. But he said, Lord, suffer me first to go and bury my father. Jesus said unto him, Let the dead bury their dead: but go thou and preach the kingdom of God."*
Luke 9:59-60

These two scriptures clearly show that Jesus is interested in preaching the kingdom of God to the living, rather than performing the last earthly rites to the dead or praying for the deceased

"...God is not the God of the dead, but of the living."
Matthew 22:32

Based on the information provided, Christians should not go before the presence of God at His Throne of Grace as intercessors for those who have passed on.

It is imperative that Christians pray with sincere intensity for our unsaved family, friends and associates while they live. Testify to them of Jesus while they are alive. Spread His Gospel to them while they live. Encourage them to become baptized believers while they live. When night comes (death), you will not be able to share the Gospel or pray for your unsaved loved ones. Therefore, it is useless to pray for departed loved ones. Only 'The Judgment' will tell whether or not departed loved ones are saved.

6) Are we supposed to make requests to God?
Coretha, Homewood, Illinois

Absolutely, a request to God is called a petition prayer. Your petitions or requests to God are exactly what He wants you to do when you communicate in His presence, at His Throne of Grace. He wants you to tell Him your troubles, joys, needs and desires.

"Be careful for nothing; but in everything by prayer and supplication with thanksgiving let your requests be made known unto God."
Philippians 4:6

As indicted in the previous question some things should not be requested. Nevertheless, every request made must be in the will of God for a positive response.

"And this is the confidence that we have in him, that, if we ask anything according to His will, He heareth us: And if we know that He hear us, whatsoever we ask, we know that we have the petitions that we desired of Him."
1ˢᵗ John 5:14-15

Read this verse carefully. It clearly states that:

1) We must have confidence in God when we pray.

   "And this is the confidence that we have in him...."

2) We must ask *(petition)* according to His will.

   "...that, if we ask anything according to His will,..."

252

3)   if we petition according to His will,
       "...He hears us."

4)   therefore, with all confidence we know
       that whatever we ask in His will, He will
       grant it.
       "...And if we know that He hear us,
       Whatsoever we ask, we know that we have
       the petitions that we desired of Him. ..."

A Prayer of Praise Adoration and Petition

Our Father, my Lord and my God bless Your Holy Name, O Lord, for giving me good counsel. I Thank You my God. Father, God in heaven, when I in awesome wonder consider all the world Your hands have made and how You have allowed me to dwell in the beauty of Your splendor, I cannot help but praise Your name. Day and night, at noon time and evening, I call out to You and You hear me. You answer my prayers. Thank You for Your truth. Thank You for Your righteousness. Thank You for Your peace. Thank You for the faith You have given me. Thank You for saving me from eternal death and destruction. Thank You for Your word. Help me to learn and apply it in my life daily. Thank You for the Whole Armor of God You have given us. Thank You for the seven basic applications recorded in this book to be used for establishing good prayer habits. Thank You for Your everlasting love. Thank You O Lord God my Father for all Your blessings. Thank You for a mind willing to make these applications an active part of my life. All praises, honor and glory to You in the name of Your Son, our Lord and Savior, Jesus Christ.

Amen

Conclusion

"Let us hear the conclusion of the whole matter:
Fear God, and keep his commandments: for this
is the whole duty of man."
Ecclesiastes 12:13

The basic elements for having the ear of God when we pray have been indicated in this book as follows:

1) Know what prayer is,
2) Know the purpose of prayer,
3) Realize that there are no specific types or postures for prayer,
4) Know that right motives and attitudes are essential for prayer,
5) Know that God answers prayer,
6) Know the basic hindrances to prayer,
7) Understand the Model Prayer,
8) Develop good prayer habits,
9) Be acquainted with some benefits of prayer.

Several of these elements are innate. God has given them to every man, woman, boy and girl. They just seem to come naturally to many by the blessings and greatness of God. For others, these and many more benefits of God must be revealed. Our prayer is that this book shed some light on the blessings of God through prayer.

When we pray in the presence of God, at His Throne of Grace, God is faithful. He answers prayer. Every morning and every night as well as throughout the day, God through His Son, Jesus Christ, sends new mercies. All your needs He provides. Be faithful to Him and He will hear and answer your prayers.

For one to have perfect attendance in prayer One must attend to prayer everyday without delay.

We can all communicate with God the Creator of the Universe, through His Son, our Lord and Savior Jesus the Christ by faith, hope and trust in Him. So, pray. Pray when you feel like it. Pray when it seems that you have no feeling for prayer. Pray when rejoicing, pray when in sorrow. Just pray. Pray without ceasing, for this is the will of God.

As you conclude this reading, our prayer for you is that God may grant you His riches in glory according to His will, in His own way.

"Unto Him be glory in the church by Christ Jesus throughout all ages, world without end. Amen."

Ephesians 3:21

Sample Prayer Journal

As indicated earlier in this book, a prayer journal is an excellent means of establishing and maintaining a relationship with God through prayer. It provides a way to record His blessings. An example of a very simple journal to record your prayers and God's answers follows.

This specific prayer journal is designed with four columns:
one column to record the date of the prayer,
one column to record the essence of the prayer,
one column to record the date of the answered prayer, and
one column to record the answer to the prayer.

There is no space to track any life changing experiences because of answered prayer. It is your decision to include whatever specifics you choose to include in your own prayer journal. The one that follows is the most simplest. It was created just to get you started.

Should you choose to use a prayer journal, you will be able to reflect on the writings of your relationship with God through Jesus Christ by means of answered prayer. By doing this, you may experience joy unspeakable. How wonderful it may be to read and reflect on God's blessings to you personally.

At the end of the sample is a scripture verse that should be remembered by all who are diligently seeking a positive relationship with God through prayer. As we all know, most Christians have little communication with God unless they pray. Prayer journals can help reinforce the desired relationship with Him.

Make prayer in the presence of God
at His Throne of Grace a way of life.
Use a prayer journal.

Prayer Journal

Date	*Request*	*Date*	*Answer*

I love the Lord, because He hath heard my voice and my supplications, Because He hath inclined His ear unto me, therefore will I call upon Him as long as I live."
Psalm 116:1-2

Closing Prayer

Father God in Heaven, Holy is Your Name. Lord, You are good and Your mercies endureth forever. You are the Sovereign God of all creation. Glory to Your name. O God our Father, let Your kingdom of righteous, peace, joy in the Holy Ghost and power reign in the heart of every believer. Let Your will be done in our lives here on earth as Your will is done in Heaven. O Heavenly Father, let us submit to Your Devine Plan and Perfect Will for us as we present our bodies a living sacrifice to You. Thank You, O God and Father for Your provisions. Truly, You are gracious, righteous and kind to us. Every morning You bring new mercies to each of us. You are slow to anger and You have boundless compassion for us. Thank You, for correcting us when we need correction. Praise You O my God and Father for knowing our needs and our desires. Grant us the wisdom to make all our requests for provisions within Your will. O Lord, our God, we pour out our heart to You because You are our Salvation, our Strength and our Song. O Lord, our Lord, forgive us for all our trespasses against You. Bless us to forgive those who have trespassed against us and bless us to ask forgiveness for those we have trespassed against. Let us not hold malice or vendictiveness in our hearts. Such acts are outside of Your Perfect Will. For vengence is Yours and You said in Your word if we do not forgive others You will not forgive us. Keep us O Lord from sin. Keep us from the snares of the evil one. Lead us not into temptation, but deliver us from evil. Let us meditate on You both day and night. Bless us O God, our Father, to delight in Your word. Keep us from the paths of unrighteousness. Let the light You have given us so shine that others may see our good works, and glorify You Lord, God and Father, who art in heaven. For You are righteousness, peace, joy in the Holy Ghost and power. It is You who sustains us. It is You who provides shelter for us in the times of our storms of life. It is You, our Heavenly Father, who provides refuge in times of trouble. Thank You for supplying our every need. You are The Power. You are The Glory. You are our Eternal Hope. Praise You O Lord our Father forever and ever in the Precious Name of Jesus, Amen.

Dear reader,

May the blessings of God always be with you. Keep the faith. Read your Bible, meditate and pray. God answers prayer.

Suggested Readings

Authorized King James Version of the Holy Bible, Old and New Testaments

Alves, Elizabeth, Becoming a Prayer Warrior: A Guide to Effective and Powerful Prayer, Ventura, California, Regal Books from Gospel Light, 1998.

,The Bible Promise Book, PSI & Associates, Inc. 13322S.W.128th Street, Miami, Florida, PSI & Associates, Inc. Barbour and Company, Inc. 1985

Bounds, E. M., Thy Will Be Done, New Kensington, PA: Whitaker House, 1982.

Briscoe, D. Stuart, Getting Into God, Grand Rapids, Michigan, The Zondervan Corporation, 1975

Enyia, Samuel O., Ed.D. Creative Prayer Is Not for Showmanship, South Holland, IL. Mass Production Printing and Graphic Design, 1995.

Finney, Charles, Answers to Prayer, Minneapolis, MN: Bethany House Publishers, 1983

Finney, Charles, Principles of Prayer, Minneapolis, MN: Bethany House Publishers, 2001

George, Jim, The Remarkable Prayers of the Bible, Eugene OR., Harvest Hours Publishers, 2005

Hagin, Kenneth E., Praying To Get Results, Kenneth Hagin Ministries, 1986, P.O. Box 50126, Tulsa OK.

McIntosh, Gert, A Heart for Prayer, Uhrichsville, OH. Barbour Publishing, Inc., 2003

Merriam-Webster Online Dictionary, http://www.Merriam-Webster.com/

Munroe, Myles Dr., <u>Understanding the Purpose and Power of Prayer: Study Guide,</u> Whitaker House, 30 Hunt Valley Circle, New Kensington, PA. 15068 wwww.whitakerhouse.com

Newcombe, Jerry, <u>The Moral of the Story,</u> Broadman & Holman Publishers, Nashville, TN., 1996
<u>,One Hundred Ninety-nine Promises of God,</u> Barbour and Company, Inc. 2007

Pfeiffer, Charles, F., <u>The New Combined Bible Dictionary and Concordance</u>, Grand Rapids MI., Baker Book House, 2004

<u>,Praying God's Promises,</u> Tulsa, Oklahoma. Victory House, Inc., 1998

Richards, Clift and Kathleen, <u>Bible Prayers for all Your Needs,</u> Tulsa, Oklahoma. Victory House, Inc., 1999

James Strong, <u>Strong's Exhaustive Concordance of the Bible,</u> Crusade Bible Publishers, Inc. Nashville, TN

Richards, Clift and Kathleen, <u>Bible Prayers for all Your Needs,</u> Tulsa, Oklahoma. Victory House, Inc., 1999

Rogers, Adrian, <u>The School of Prayer</u>, Love Worth Finding Ministries, Post Office Box 38300, Memphis, TN 38183, 1-901382-7900, <u>http://www.lwf.org</u>

Strong, James, <u>Strong's Exhaustive Concordance of the Bible,</u> Crusade Bible Publishers, Inc. Nashville, TN

Wikipedia, <u>The Free Encyclopedia</u>, nwikipedia.org/wiki/ Encyclopedia

How to contact the Author

Ann Evans, a Christian Counselor, has served as a Bible school teacher, a School Guidance Counselor, an Academic Support Coordinator, and Director of Special Education. She has written numerous articles on academic study skills, Christian stewardship, and prayer.

Ann and her husband have three grown children and two lovely granddaughters. Her husband says she has great tenacity. All praises to God, she is known as the one who never gives up; but always finishes the task.

For speaking engagements, please contact the author by means of letter or Email at:

CpC Community Prayer Circle
Post Office Box 471
Attention: Author/Ann Evans
Homewood, Illinois 60430
Email:communityprayercircle@comcast.net

Personal Study Notes